*of multiculturalism*

*Sawraj Singh*

# Toward a
# Global
# Perspective

*November 27, 2005*

by

## Sawraj Singh, MD

**WORDS WORTH PRESS**
**Enterprise, Oregon**

Library of Congress Cataloging-in-Publication Data

Sawraj Singh.
Toward a global perspective / by Sawraj Singh.— 2nd ed.
p. cm.
Includes bibliographical references.
ISBN 0-915214-42-3 (alk. paper)
1. åAdi-Granth—Criticism, interpretation, etc. 2. åAdi-Granth—Philosophy. I. Title.
BL2017.45.S38 2005
294.6'17—dc22

2005018252

Second Edition

Printed and bound in the United States of America

Published by
Words Worth Press
PO Box 398
Enterprise, OR 97828
(541) 426-6095

*Cover Art by Jarnail Singh*

### Artist Statement

I strive to create images of everlasting beauty. It is a humble effort to capture on canvas the beauty and grandeur of everyday life and bountiful nature, so that it gives joy and inner peace to viewers and instills in them a sense of gratitude for the gift of life and for Nature's never ending generosity. I can paint forever the beauty of nature and the simplicity and innocence of native and indigenous cultures, which ultimately will be consumed by soulless consumerist culture in this fast changing world.

### Jarnail Singh
### Jarnail Arts 604 592 2652

Jarnail Singh also provided the cover art of *Crisis in Civilization: A Sikh Perspective* by Sawraj Singh, MD published by Words Worth Press in 2001  ISBN 0-915214-38-5

Freelancer artist, illustrator, designer, photographer and art journalist Jarnail Singh is a Sikh artist who has been painting the history and cultural traditions of his people in an effort to preserve them for the coming generations.

His works have been widely exhibited in India and abroad in one man shows and group shows. He has illustrated a number of books and magazincs covers. He is an avid photographer with many international publishing credits. The author of more than 50 articles about art and culture which have appeared in many international publications, his book "Punjabi Chitarkar" (Punjabi Painters), in Punjabi, has been published by Punjab State University Text Book Board, India.

His biography is included in school text books in my home state of Punjab in India.

# INTRODUCTION

## THE 400TH ANNIVERSARY OF GURU GRANTH SAHIB

The 400th anniversary of *Guru Granth Sahib,* the holy book of the Sikhs, falls in September, 2004. *Guru Granth Sahib* is not only the holy book for the Sikhs, but is also a great source of spiritual knowledge, comprehensive philosophy of life, and provides a global perspective. Therefore, I want to dedicate this book to the 400th anniversary of *Guru Granth Sahib.* I feel this is a great opportunity for the Sikh community to give correct information about the Sikhs and their philosophy. The message of *Guru Granth Sahib* is not limited to the Sikhs but is for the unification and salvation of all mankind. This message is based upon universal concern and universal well being.

This is also a golden opportunity for the whole of mankind to learn about the only truly multi-cultural holy book. Therefore, it can provide a global perspective which is needed to form the ideological basis for the emerging new world order, a multi-polar world. The biggest challenge faced by the contemporary world is the lack of a global perspective. This can foster ethical globalization rather than a globalization which is purely economic. The universal outlook and the global perspective of *Guru Granth Sahib* can help resolve this major contradiction.

*Guru Granth Sahib* is the essence and the zenith of Eastern cultivational spirituality. *Guru Granth Sahib* provides us with *Brahm Gian* (spiritual knowledge) and *Tat Gian* (essence of knowledge, or spiritual wisdom), the experience of the True Self. By this we become aware that we are part of the whole, the Ultimate Reality, which can also be called Eternal Truth. *Guru Granth Sahib* deals with only spiritual knowledge. There is no ritualism in it. The message of *Guru Granth Sahib* is simple and clear so that all people can easily understand it.

The message of *Guru Granth Sahib* is not abstract, but it is a practical philosophy which deals with human and social evolution. The human evolution is not detached from social practice but social interaction is an integral part for our salvation. According to the traditional Indian philosophy there are four pillars of our life. These are called *dharma, arth, kam,* and *mokash.* Meaning respectively duty, economics, passions, and means to salvation. *Guru Granath Sahib* deals with all the four aspects of life. These four aspects are not addressed in a fragmented manner but are addressed in totality. On one hand, human development is associated with natural law and harmony with nature, while on the other hand it also deals with social issues of fairness, equality, human rights, and respect for women.

Capitalism and Marxism seem to be promoting a philosophy of conquering nature whereas *Guru Granth Sahib* emphasizes the concept of living in harmony with nature. Both of these modern philosophies, capitalism and Marxism, seem to give the impression that human values are not permanent but keep changing with time. They also seem to promote the idea that human beings reached their highest level of development in the modern age and people became wisest in the post modern age. *Guru Granth Sahib* gives the message that human values are timeless: respect for nature, harmony with nature, principles of restraint and moderation, and living according to *hukam* (the universal order), which can be understood as living in a state of equilibrium with nature. *Guru Granth Sahib* promotes the concept of natural evolution as opposed to the concepts of imposed development of capitalism and Marxism. The basic concepts of capitalism can be challenged by the fact that in the last two centuries, under their influence, we have not become better human beings and the world has not become a better or safer place. Many of us will also agree that the benefits of development in the last two centuries have not been shared by the vast majority of people of the world. Maybe time has come to try another philosophy to meet the challenges before us. *Guru Granth Sahib* offers us an alternative form of development. We can merge eastern wisdom with western science and technology. This can help both the East and the West.

The Indian traditional thought offered three paths to salvation. These are *karma, gian,* and *bhakti* (meaning actions, knowledge, and devotion, respectively). The priestly (Brahmanical) class tried to interpret these concepts in a self-serving manner. Karma, which means actions or efforts, was converted from an active concept to passive and fatalistic concepts of *karamkand,* or ritualism. A person had to reap the fruits or payback for the karmas accumulated in previous incarnations. There was not much he could do to change his fate except let the priestly class perform rituals to free him from accumulated karma. Guru Nanak reiterated active interpretation of karma as *kirat,* which means honest and productive work. *Gian* (knowledge) was monopolized by the priestly class. Sanskrit was used as the language for spiritual knowledge. This was not understood by ordinary people. Guru Nanak advocated *nam japo* (spiritual awakening for everybody). All people gained access to spiritual knowledge because this was made available in their language, the language they could understand. *Bhakti,* which means devotion, was also misinterpreted by the priestly class. The essence of devotion is love. But the priestly class emphasized the ritual aspect rather than love. Guru Nanak preached the third fundamental principle of Sikhism: *Wand chako,* which means sharing your good fortune. Sharing means love. There is a difference between love and attachment. Love is based on sharing or giving, while attachment tries to hold on to somebody. *Guru Granth Sahib* explains the three basic principles of the Sikh philosophy: *kirat karo* (engage in honest and productive work), *nam japo* (enlighten yourself spiritually), and *wand chako* (share your good fortune). These are principles of human develop- ment as well as for developing an ideal society, because without spiritual awakening an ideal society cannot be built.

*Guru Granth Sahib* is an open dialogue. It does not advocate only one path to reach ultimate reality or eternal truth. *Guru Granth Sahib* is a true representation of diversity and pluralism. It emphasizes realization of our true self by means of love and knowledge. So long as our ultimate goal is the same it allows you freedom of choosing your path. *Guru Granth Sahib* does not try to convert people to the Sikh religion, but preaches to make all people better human beings. The Hindus should become better Hindus and the Muslims better Muslims. Similarly, the Christians and Jews should become better Christians and better Jews. In the end, I feel that the 400th anniver- sary of this great holy book should be a celebration of love, tolerance, peaceful coexistence, diversity, pluralism, universal concern, univer- sal well being, and universal brotherhood. These principles are the ingredients for developing a global perspective and a new world order of genuine universal peace, freedom, and shared prosperity of authentic well beings.

# CHAPTER ONE

## CULTIVATIONAL AND PRESCRIPTIVE SPIRITUALITY

Spirituality is primarily of two types, cultivational and prescriptive. The cultivational spirituality stresses the inner development of spirituality. It takes into account individual variation. The prescriptive spirituality seeks direction from outside. It is more collective and cannot easily accommodate individual differences. In Eastern spirituality, the cultivational aspect is dominant, whereas in Western spirituality, the prescriptive aspect dominates. The Eastern religions, such as Hinduism, Jainism, Buddhism and Sikhism, emphasize cultivational spirituality. The Judeo-Semitic religions, Judaism, Christianity and Islam, lay more emphasis on the prescriptive aspect of spirituality. Out of the Judeo-Semitic religions, Islam had the closest contact with Eastern religions. Therefore Islam, particularly the Sufi sect of Islam, is very much influenced by the cultivational spirituality of the East.

The different approaches of the Eastern and Judeo-Semitic religions towards spirituality are primarily the result of different climatic conditions. All major Eastern religions, Hinduism, Jainism,

Buddhism, and Sikhism arose in the Indian subcontinent. The climate in the Indian subcontinent was very mild and there was abundant vegetation. An individual could easily survive in the wild and could devote all the time to one's individual spiritual growth. In the Indian tradition, there are words like *Arnayak* and *Sanyas*. The word *Arnayak* means wandering in the jungle and the word *Sanyas* means renunciation. *Arnayak* can also mean preliminary knowledge and *Upanishad* means conclusive knowledge. Not only ordinary people retreated into the jungle for their spiritual uplift, but many kings also renounced their kingdoms and moved to the jungle after taking *sanyas*.

Judeo-Semitic religions arose in a much harsher climate of the desert. At the time of their origin, people were still primarily nomadic. The concept of retreat and individual spiritual uplift was not very practical under those circumstances. For an individual to be able to survive, he had to stick to the tribe. This resulted in evolving a more collective approach. The subservience of the individual to the collective (tribe) led to clearly drawn directions for prescriptive spirituality. Guru Nanak used the word *Kateb* for Judeo-Semitic religions. The word *Kateb* means a book of rules and directions, in other words prescriptive spirituality. The adherents of Judaism, Christianity, and Islam have been singularly characterized as "people of the Book," that is the Torah, the Bible, and the Koran, each of which is deemed to have been prescribed from God.

The division between the Eastern cultivational and the Western prescriptive spiritualities is not watertight. Both have elements of each other incorporated in them. There is a concept of retreat in Christianity and Ramadan in Islam. Both of these can be called cultivational. Similarly, the ritualistic aspect of Hinduism in which reciting *mantras* (hymns and spells), performing *Yaggas* (ritualistic sacrifices), *Havan* (fire worship), *Tirath* (holy pilgrimage), and *Ishnan* (spiritually cleansing bath) can also all be called prescriptive because they are all regulated by strict rules. In spite of this overlapping, the fact remains that the Eastern spirituality is primarily cultivational and the Western spirituality is primarily prescriptive.

The cultivational spirituality is mainly based on knowledge *(Gian)* which helps us to understand ourselves and our surroundings. The ultimate stage of development of knowledge can be called *Brahm Gian* (highest spiritual knowledge). It can also be called *Tat Gian* (essence of knowledge) or *Vastvic Gian* (real knowledge). At this stage of knowledge there is complete self-realization, where a person realizes that he is part of the whole. The prescriptive spirituality is mainly based on faith. Spirituality, both Eastern and Western, have to have both knowledge and faith. The Eastern cultivational spirituality emphasizes that knowledge ultimately leads to faith, whereas Western prescriptive spirituality believes that faith will lead to knowledge. I feel, in cultivational spirituality faith is evolved, while in prescriptive spirituality faith is imposed.

Guru Nanak, the founder of the Sikh religion, preached that there is only one source of creation for all men, planets, and the universe. Therefore, there is only one true reality. It is a curtain of ignorance which makes us believe we are separate from others. Chronologically, the Sikh religion is the last major religion to develop in the Indian subcontinent. Due to this, the Sikh religion gained an opportunity to study other religions as well as other ideologies. It studied the formative aspects of the other religions and was able to develop those concepts further. The Sikh religion clarified and simplified them so ordinary people can understand them better. By using Punjabi, which was the language of the people, this purpose was easily served.

If we try to analyze the evolution of Indian thought, one fact becomes obvious. There were two main tendencies existing in the tradition of spiritual evolution; the first is known as *Brahm Gian,* which means the highest spiritual knowledge and the other is known as *Karamkand,* meaning rituals. Buddhism and Jainism primarily emphasized knowledge. In the Buddhist religion, Buddha, the highest spiritually developed person, means an enlightened person. According to them, knowledge alone can lead to liberation. Neither Buddhism nor Jainism accepted the authority of the Vedas, but they have promoted concepts of cultivational spirituality.

The concept of not believing in God was a deviation from traditional Indian thought. The *Rig Veda,* which laid the foundation of the Indian thought, had emphasized the concept of God. *Bhagavad*

*Gita* is a holy book which deals with the essence of knowledge. Then, a priestly class emerged which promoted rituals and deviated from *Brahm Gian*. At this juncture, Jainism and Buddhism emerged. They were opposed to ritualism and monopoly of the priestly class. They wanted to reemphasize knowledge, *Brahm gian*. Buddhism spread widely in India and became the state religion. Under the great king Ashoka, Buddhism flourished in India. Buddhism also spread to China, Japan, Korea, and Southeast Asia, and became the major religion of Asia.

Slowly, ritualism crept back into Buddhism. The original Buddhism, Hinayana, (see Theravada as a particular offshoot) was modified as Mahayana (the Great Vehicle).

A priestly class started to reemerge. Next, Buddhism introduced Tantric Buddhism (the so-called left and right hand paths, both emphasizing rites and rituals; consult Tantra). The priestly class degenerated further into a second rate Brahmanical class. Then came a Hindu (Vedic) revival. Shankaracharya, (one of India's most well known saints and philosophers, 788-820 c.e.) from south India, led the movement to revive *Brahm gian* and struggle against ritualistic domination. Shankaracharya went all over India and engaged other scholars in debates and discussions, spreading the message of *Brahm gian*. This led to revival of the Vedic religion. The Tantric Buddhism could not withstand this Vedic revival. Then came the armed onslaught of Muslim invasion. This gave the final blow to an already weakened Buddhism in India. Buddhism was almost completely wiped out from the Indian subcontinent although it flourished in the rest of Asia.

This Sufi movement in India was different than the Sufi movement in the Middle East which was born of Islam. Many believe the Sufi movement in India was the result of the influence of Hinduism on Islam.

There was interaction between the Hindu and the Muslim religions. The impact of Islam on Hinduism gave rise to a new movement called Bhakti, meaning a devotional movement. (Bhakti is one of the principal variants of yoga in the great Indian tradition.) This interaction between Hindu and Muslim religions tried to bring together the good points of both. The Hindu religion in turn reacted to Islam, leading to the Sufi movement in India. Sufis were the mystics of Islam. The Sikh religion can be considered the climax of the Bhakti movement.

The Sikh religion was also influenced by the Sufi movement. The Sikh holy book,*Guru Granth Sahib,* has writings of the Bhakti and Sufi mystics as well as the Sikh gurus. Guru Nanak, while emphasizing the importance of spiritual knowledge, also stressed the role of love as the main path of uniting with God. He described God as a timeless and constant creator who is formless and infinite. This is the transcendent aspect of God. But God is both transcendent and immanent *(Nirgun* and *Sargun)* respectively. The immanent aspect of God is manifested in nature. Guru Nanak preached love, tolerance, peaceful coexistence, universal concern and universal well-being. Guru Nanak had a universal outlook and a global perspective. Guru Nanak was a great advocate of dialogue, pluralism, and diversity. These principles form the basis of multiculturalism.

The principles of the Sikh religion are very relevant and important for mankind and the world. We have a major contradiction in the world today. On the one hand, we have evolved into a global community, but on the other hand, we have been unable to develop a global perspective. Guru Nanak's message can provide that global perspective which is very much needed and can help to resolve this contradiction peacefully. The Western prescriptive spirituality has been unable to meet the challenges of the Western society because the political and social systems promote individualism, whereas the prescriptive spirituality has a collective approach.

This situation has created a spiritual vacuum. The Eastern cultivational spirituality can help fill this vacuum.

Historically, the Indian subcontinent has been the main seat for the development of cultivational spirituality. I believe Guru Nanak's message and the Sikh religion should be seen as the essence of the Eastern cultivational spirituality and the highest developed form of Indian thought. The evolution of Indian thought should be seen as a continuous phenomenon starting from the Vedic period to the evolution of the Sikh religion in the shape of a pyramid, where the Vedic religion forms the base and the Sikh religion forms the peak.

The cultivational spirituality is an evolved form of spirituality whereas the prescriptive spirituality is an imposed form. I believe anything which is evolved is superior to anything which is imposed. Both the Eastern and Judeo-Semitic religions have elements of both cultivational and prescriptive spirituality. We have to remember that all the major religions have originated in Asia; therefore, they are Eastern in origin. The difference in cultivational and prescriptive aspects is primarily due to geographical and climatic conditions. The geographical and climatic conditions of the Indian subcontinent were very conducive for the development of the cultivational spirituality.

The most fundamental concept of the Eastern cultivational spirituality is the concept of an inward journey of self-realization as the main instrument for spiritual elevation: from physical existence, to mental flight, to the realm of the soul; from outer-self to inner-self and finally to the true self. The outer-self is our physical self, composed of five elements. They are called *Panj bhooti* (five elements). These are earth, water, fire, air and space, called *prithivi, jal, agni, vayu,* and *akash.* The physical is most basic and also considered the lowest level of existence. Then comes our inner-self, called *antakaran.* This is composed of *man* (mind), *buddhi* (intellect), *chit* (consciousness), and *ahankar* (ego). The mind, intellect, and our memory give us impressions of our inner-self, but this is ego which is not our real or true self. To reach our true self we have to transcend our mind, intellect, memory, and ego. This state is the ultimate level of self-realization and the highest level of our existence. We are residing in the realm of soul. The soul is called *Jeevatma*(individual soul as microcosm) and God is *Paramatma* (supreme soul as macrocosm). They can be compared to a drop of water and an ocean. One is small and the other is very large but the difference is only in size. Both have water as their content. When a drop of water merges with the water of the ocean nobody can differentiate between the water of the drop or of the ocean. Therefore, differences between nature and God are only in form—the content is the same. Once we realize our content or essence, then we unite with God; in other words, our existence becomes cosmic and universal. This content or essence is called *Mool Tat* (fundamental essence).

The ultimate goal of self-realization is recognizing one's *Mool tat.* The transcendent God, *Parbrahm Parmatma* is formless and no qualities can be attributed to it. This is called *Nirgun.* Nature, on the other hand, has form and has qualities. This is the immanent aspect of God to which we can attribute qualities. It is called *Sargun.* The difference in the transcendent aspect of God *(Parmatma)* and the immanent aspect of God (nature) is only in the form; the content is the same.

The qualities are called *Gunas.* Since we are parts of the immanent aspect of God, (nature) we have qualities *(gunas).* There are three qualities. All human beings have these three qualities in them. These qualities are *rajo, tamas,* and *sato.* These are names of colors. *Rajo* means red, *tamas* means black (dark), and *sato* means white. Roughly, they mean different orientations of a person. *Rajo* represents passions, excitement and drive. *Tamas* means the dark side of life such as lust, greed, lethargy, and gluttony. *Sato* personifies what are considered good qualities like patience, balance, stability, and compassion. All the three *gunas* are present in each person but people differ from one another based on which *guna* is dominant in them. Originally, the castes were created on the basis of these *gunas.* Those who had domination of *sato* were called Brahmins, created from the head of God, (at the top of the caste system). *Kasatriyas* were people with dominance of *rajo,* created from the hand of God, (the ruler and warrior class next in line). *Sudras,* created from the feet of God (mostly artisans and laborers were the lowest, except for the "untouchables," who had no caste status), were supposed to have domination of *tamas. Vaishyas* were created from the stomach of God, in between *sudras* and *kashatriyas,* having dominance of *rajo* and *tamas* combined (being business and trade persons and third in rank). Later on, as the caste system degenerated, people were not divided into castes based on their qualities but were divided on the basis of their birth.

Guru Nanak preached that in order to unite with God we have to rise above the three qualities *(tregun ateet).* As long as we are attached to any of these qualities we have not realized our real self. Our real self is part of the whole, it is not separate from the ultimate reality, which is timeless truth and identical with the constant creator.

In other words, we are seeing nature (creation) separate from God (creator). This means parallelism and dualism. Guru Nanak condemned all forms of parallelism and dualism as ignorance and delusion; because they prevent us from realizing our true self and uniting us with the ultimate reality which is our liberation and our salvation. Only by dissolving our false identity *(Hamay)* can we realize our true identity, *mool tat* (fundamental essence).

Guru Nanak discarded the caste system because it is based on *gunas,* (qualities of nature) or the form, while the essence is only one. This means that the differences between human beings are superficial as they only exist in the outer form, while the essence is the same light which shines in each of us. Guru Nanak asked, "how can men be different and separated when the same light shines in all of them?" This principle is the basis of Guru Nanak's message of the unity of mankind.

Another concept of cultivational spirituality is the concept of *koshas. Koshas* are like sheaths of our personality as we travel from the outside to the core. The first sheath is called *aan mai kosh,* which means elemental existence, existence limited to the physical self. The second *kosh* is *pran mai kosh*, or ethereal existence, when a person becomes aware of *prana,* the energy which flows through us. The third *kosh* is called *man mai kosh,* the level of mental flight. The fourth *kosh* is called *viggyan mai kosh,* meaning scientific knowledge. The fifth *kosh* is called *anand mai kosh.* This is the state of equipoise and bliss. This is the state of the inner core.

The state of supreme bliss comes from a state of equipoise, which means realizing your true self and being in a state of harmony with nature and the universe. Supreme bliss is called *paramanand* and supreme status is called *parampad.* Guru Nanak preached that *paramanand* (supreme bliss) and *parampad* (supreme status) are activated by uniting with the One. When there is no feeling of duality *(dooj),* ignorance *(bharam)* is removed. In other words, by recognizing one's true self (one's fundamental essence) and becoming aware of the fact that one is part of the whole and there is only one ultimate reality. One is part of that universal reality like everything else. Ignorance of this reality causes fear, anxiety, separation, and suffering.

Awareness of universal oneness leads to alleviation of all this suffering, and leads one to eternal and supreme bliss.

The concept of chakras is also based on the philosophy of cultivational spirituality, which means elevating yourself from the lower centers to higher centers. There are seven chakras. Five of the chakras correspond to the five basic elements, earth, water, fire, air and space. The sixth chakra corresponds to mind and intellect. The seventh chakra elevates us to cosmic awareness. Therefore, they follow the basic concept of elevating one's existence from body to mind and finally to the soul (from physical to mental to spiritual).

The first chakra is called *muladhara* and corresponds with the earth *(prithivi)* element which means basic survival. This is the lowest chakra residing in the lowest part of the spine. The second chakra corresponds to water *(jal)*. This is at the level of the genitals, meaning procreation. Water is in the sperm and ovum. The third chakra corresponds to fire *(agni)*. This is called *manipura* or *nabh* (umbilicus). *Agni* represents passion. The fourth chakra is called *anahata* or *hridaya* (heart) chakra. This corresponds to the air element. The heart is surrounded by the lungs. The lungs have air in them. This chakra represents compassion. The fifth chakra is called *vishuddha* or *kanth* (throat) chakra. This corresponds to the space *(akash)* element. With our voice we can communicate with others (express our compassion). The sixth chakra is called the *aagya* chakra. This is on the forehead and corresponds with mind and intellect. The seventh chakra corresponds to *dashamdavar,* which translates into the tenth gate.

*Pranayam* is a form of yoga which is based on controlling your breathing. There is another concept in yoga of achieving the blissful state by reaching a balance between the moon and the sun channels. The left nostril (irha) is considered the moon channel and the right nostril (pingala) is considered the sun channel. The sun channel is also called the fire (agni) channel, meaning passion and drive. The moon channel is cooling or calming. In between these channels lies *sukhman,* meaning blissful channel. This travels in the middle of these channels, along the spine to the brain. It is also called *Brahm marg* (spiritual path) or *maha marg* (great path).

There are nine natural orifices in the body. They are called *davars* or gates: two eyes, two ears, two nostrils, one mouth, one genital orifice (penis in the male and vagina in the female) and anus (rectum). Sikhs believe the tenth orifice is a hidden orifice or gate on the top of the head through which we are connected to the cosmos and the universe. Some people call it *jayotiroop singhasan* which means throne of light. Light is a universal symbol of knowledge. The concept regarding this chakra is that those people who can elevate or cultivate their spiritual selves to the highest level can reside at the level of this chakra and open the tenth gate. After this gate opens, we can reach a cosmic and universal existence.

The spiritual elevation means moving from the lower centers to the higher centers. The basic instincts try to pull us down by inciting the five messengers of wickedness; *kam* (lust), *krodh* (anger), *lobh* (greed), *moh* (false attachment), and *ahankar* (arrogance). Our soul, the highest center, tries to pull us up by controlling these five messengers of wickedness.

We should also try to understand the concepts of false attachment and positive detachment. The false attachment *(moh)* is considered one of the messengers of wickedness. *Moh,* false attachment, is the result of ignorance. It fails to understand different levels of reality. It sees perceptive reality as the ultimate reality. It does not differentiate between the transient *(anit)* and permanent *(nit)*. It also cannot see the difference between destructible *(nashwar)* and indestructible *(shashwat)*.

The first false attachment we make is with our own body. We do not stay the same. Our body is constantly changing. William Shakespeare's poem "Seven Ages of Man" outlines how the body keeps changing from an infant to an old man. We also try to ignore the simple fact that, as far as the body is concerned, the only final truth is death. Every living organism which is born has to die. The false attachment with the body is the main cause of *duhkha* (suffering). Understanding this basic fact led the prince Sidhartha to enlightenment and he became Buddha. He saw how people became sick, old, and died. His father had kept him in a secluded palace where nobody old, ugly, or sick was allowed to go. He was always surrounded by beautiful and young people. One day Sidhartha managed to see the real world where there were old and sick people. People died. The young handsome prince was shocked. He realized he would also become old and that one day he would die. He could also become sick. The prince realized he was living a life of false attachment which in the end would only result in *duhkha* (suffering). He wanted to find a way out of this suffering. He gave up his kingdom, left his beautiful wife and son behind, and went into the jungle to find a way out of this suffering. The intense search made him enlightened and he became Buddha (awakened). He found that only real knowledge can emancipate you from suffering. Many years later, when he returned to his home city, his wife, his son and the rest of his family became his followers in the search for that real knowledge. Thousands of other people followed and they were called *Bhikshus,* which translates into seekers of knowledge.

The *Bhagavad-Gita* gives a very clear message of positive detachment. It says we should detach from ourselves and look upon ourselves as *Drashtas,* meaning observers. Only in this way can we maintain a perfect balanced state called *Sam Awastha.* If we do not detach ourselves, then we will remain in a perpetual state of *raga* or *divesha,* meaning attraction and repulsion as love and hate. If we become observers and remain in *Samawastha* (balanced state) then our actions become devotional and can unite us with God. This is called *Karam Yoga.* The word yoga means union. This union is between *Jeevatma* (individual soul) with *Parmatma* (supreme soul). There are many forms of yoga but Krishna says that if you perform your actions without worrying about the results *(Nishkam Karam).* Then they become *karam yoga.* If we understand that it is our duty to put in efforts but results are not in our hands, then we act with the feeling that we are doing our duty and results are in the hands of God. This is the highest form of yoga. *Karam yoga* is even superior to *karma sanyasi* (the one who is a renunciate).

Guru Nanak develops the concept of positive detachment to the highest level. Guru Nanak preached that if we attach ourselves to transitory and impermanent things, then we will only get suffering. If we want to obtain supreme bliss, we have to attach ourselves to eternal truth (ultimate reality). This eternal truth is timeless, has no beginning and no end. It is a formless constant creator and it creates itself. To attach to the eternal truth (ultimate reality) we have to detach ourselves from the three qualities *(treguna)* of *rajo, tamo,* and *sato.* This state is called *Tregun Ateet* (free of the three qualities) because these three qualities lead us to false attachments *(moh)* and *moh* will lead to ignorance, delusion, and suffering.

Some may question why we should give up *sato gun* because they are good qualities. This story will probably illustrate the importance of freeing ourselves from the three qualities if we want our salvation. A *rishi* is in deep meditation in a jungle. A hunter kills a doe near him. The orphaned baby deer is adopted by the *rishi.* The *rishi* gets so attached to the fawn that he is constantly worried about the deer. If he does not see the deer then he starts thinking that some hunting animal might have eaten it. The *rishi* could not concentrate on his meditation. This act motivated by a *sato gun* of compassion distracted the *rishi* from his main purpose and defeated the very purpose of his being in the jungle.

Where did the *rishi* go wrong? Was it wrong to take care of the baby deer? Where he went wrong was when he overstepped his duty. He is worried about the result, whether the deer will live or not. Who lives or not is determined by somebody else. The *rishi* should have done his job and let Him do his job. That is what is called *Nishkam Karam* (detached action). Attachments will lead to anxiety, fear, and suffering.

The positive detachment is also called *Vairag.* The word *Maya* means illusion and material reality at the same time. If is true that the material reality around us was created by the same creator who has created us, then how can it be an illusion? It becomes illusion when we do not differentiate between different levels of reality. *Maya* can be perceptive or preliminary reality, but when we start considering it the final or ultimate reality, it becomes an illusion. Guru Nanak warns us that we should not get tangled with *maya.* In other words, do not misunderstand the perceptive and preliminary reality as the final and ultimate reality. If we do this, we will be lost and this will result in pain and suffering. We will be unable to reach salvation.

*Vairag* means detachment from maya, but does that mean we have to deny or separate ourselves from the material reality around us? Guru Nanak preaches that we do not have to renounce the material reality around us, but while living in it we can still detach ourselves from it. Guru Nank gives an example of the lotus flower which lives in water but still stays above it. You can compare a lotus flower with a frog: the lotus flower stays unaffected by the water and the mud, while the frog is affected by both. Similarly, some people can be part of society but are not affected by corruption and pollution while others cannot resist them. For *Vairag,* Guru Nanak does not want you to leave society but stay in it in a state of positive detachment—like the lotus flower. Guru Nanak preached that *Sanyas* (renunciation) is possible by living with the family, that is called *Garisth.*

Our mind is the main mode for making false attachments. Mind is always wandering; it cannot stay still. Mind does not stay focused on the present. It is either jumping to the future *(kalpana)* or ruminating over the past *(Simriti).* Mind has also been compared to an unbridled horse, or even to a monkey which cannot sit still and is always jumping around. The primary role of cultivational spirituality is to bring the mind under control of the higher centers. There are different ways to achieve this. Guru Nanak's path is of knowledge and love. With knowledge, we understand the eternal truth or ultimate reality, and with love we unite with that reality. As long as we are united with that reality we stay focused and are in a state of equipoise, which is called *Sahaj.* Then we are in a state of supreme bliss *(param anand).* When we are separated from the eternal truth, then we become vulnerable to anxiety and fear which lead to pain and suffering.

One form of mind control, yoga, has become popular in the West. I feel yoga has been promoted more as a Jane Fonda or aerobic exercise as a health and fitness tool rather than a comprehensive philosophy of cultivational spirituality. Yoga *(shastar)* was one of the six schools of the Indian philosophy. It was started by Rishi Patanjali. *Shastaras* are schools of Indian philosophy based on the *Vedas.* They are part of the Hindu scriptures. The word yoga means union. This union between *Jeevatma* (individual soul) and *paramatma* (supreme soul) is achieved by reaching the state where all activities of mind stop. This state of mind is called *Chitvirti Norodh.* There are five states of mind. These are called *Chit Bhumi.* The first state is called *Kaspit* when mind is active and is wandering around external objects. The second is called *Mudh,* when mind is in a sleep-like state. The third state is *Vikipsat* when mind becomes relatively quiet and peaceful. The fourth state is *Ikagarta,* when mind is focused. The fifth state is called *Nirudh,* when all activities of mind cease. There are eight steps of yoga, which are called *yogang* (parts of yoga). *Yam,* or *Sanjam,* means those things we should not be doing. *Niyam* means moral principles which we should follow. *Asan* means posture, *Pranayam* means controlling your breathing, *Paratiker* means controlling your senses, and *dharna* means focusing your mind on some internal part or external object. *Dhian* means meditation. *Samadhi* means that state of focusing and concentration achieved by meditation when there is no difference (separation) between the person who is meditating and the object of his meditation. This means that *jeevatma* has united with *paramatma.*

The words Guru and Sikh have become familiar to most of the people in the West. Guru is a Punjabi word for teacher. Sikh is a Punjabi word for student. The Sanskrit word *Shiskardick* also means student. The word guru is derived from two Sanskrit words, *Gu* and *Ru. Gu* means darkness and *ru* means light. Guru is the one who pulls you out of darkness into light. Darkness and light are universal symbols of ignorance and knowledge. The word guru also implies that knowledge is our teacher. Guru Nanak uses the word Sikh for his followers because they should continue to learn all their lives. Learning is a never-ending phenomenon and should be a life-long process. Guru Nanak also preached that humility is the best virtue. Humility and knowledge reside together. Similarly, arrogance and ignorance always accompany each other. The Sikh should always remind us that we have more to learn and should help us remain humble.

Prescriptive and cultivational spirituality are different means to achieve the same end, which is, to make a person better. Religions are also different paths which we can follow to reach the same **destination**, the eternal truth, the ultimate reality. Guru Nanak was once asked which religion was better, Hinduism or the Islam, to which he replied that what really matters is that one becomes a better person. The same thing can be said about different forms of spirituality. However, one fact should be emphasized, that consumer culture has practically killed spirituality and we need all the help we can get from anywhere to fill this spiritual vacuum. The Western prescriptive spirituality has to be supplemented by the Eastern cultivational spirituality. Otherwise, spiritual revival has no chance.

I was born in Punjab, India and I have lived in America for more than 30 years. From what I could learn from both societies I feel there are many principles and values which are shared by both Eastern and Western societies. Therefore, there are shared and common concepts in prescriptive and cultivational spiritualities. This commonality proves that there are universal values. I want to share my impressions about these, what I believe are universal values.

**Faith**. Whatever is happening, is happening as a part of the universal order and this is happening for our good.

**Optimism.** Whatever is going to happen is also going to happen according to His will (universal will) and will be good for us. Guru Nanak calls this universal order *Hukam.*

**Humility.** Humility is a virtue while arrogance is a vice.

**Patience.** Patience is a universally recognized value.

**Restraint.** Restraint or moderation is revered by all cultures.

**Compassion.** We should be compassionate to all people, living organisms, and non-living objects. (Do not pollute the earth, air, or water.)

**Sympathy.** Be helpful to everybody.

**Effort.** We should put sincere efforts to achieve our goals.

**Courage.** We should not be discouraged regardless of the results of our efforts, and we should have the courage to face consequences of our actions.

**Balance.** We should try to maintain our balance under all circumstances.

**Equality.** We should treat other people as equal to us.

**Calmness.** We should not be provoked or become angry.

**Fearlessness.** If we believe that there is a universal order and everything is happening according to that order  for our good, then why should we be afraid?

**Give up anxiety.** We are always worried about what is going to happen to us. If everything which is going to happen is according to His will (part of a higher order) then why should we worry?

**Give up jealousy.** Everybody gets what they deserve. Therefore, why should we be jealous?

**Give up slander.** The only person you can change is yourself. If you keep criticizing others then you loose the chance of improving yourself.

**Knowledge.** Give up ignorance and superstition, and become enlightened.

In this era of globalization without a global perspective, these universal values have been suppressed. Instead of these, we are encouraged to seek instant gratification and climb the ladder of success—no matter how many people we have to step on. If we want to bring a global perspective to this globalization then we have to promote these universal values. Guru Nanak had a global perspective and universal outlook. His message becomes very relevant and important.

# CHAPTER TWO

## LINEAR AND MULTI-LAYERED APPROACHES

The word linear means in relation to length only; in other words, using just one dimension. In layman's terminology this term is commonly described as having a one-track mind. As opposed to a linear approach, the multi-layered approach is multi-dimensional. It tries to view a phenomenon from many aspects. This approach tries to understand the inter-relationship between different things and phenomena. A multi-layered approach is more comprehensive than the linear approach, and it can help us understand reality better. Generally, the linear approach makes us less tolerant to other people's views and has a tendency to impose our perspective on others. The linear approach also leads to an attempt at conquering rather than coexisting.

The linear approach has been more prevalent in the West and the multi-layered approach was more popular in the east. The difference can be even seen in the evolution of Western and Eastern thoughts. For the West, there has been a tendency that at one time only one school of thought became dominant while another replaced it. This phenomenon is also called succession. In the East, on the other hand, different schools of thought coexisted and flourished. A good example is evolution of six schools of Indian philosophy called *Shastras*. These six schools of Indian philosophy not only differed from each other, but they also had opposing views. Yet they coexisted and flourished together. They often held discussions and hotly debated contested issues, but were still able to maintain harmony.

Not only in philosophy, but even in medicine, the differences in the linear and multi-layered approaches become apparent. In the ancient Indian society and in contemporary Indian society, different schools of medicine have coexisted. Along with Western allopathic medicine, one sees other schools of medicine flourishing in India. These include *Ayurvedic* medicine, *Hikmat* medicine, based on Islamic and Greek (called *Unani* in India) concepts, homeopathic and herbal medicine. In Delhi, India's capital, ultramodern hospitals and *Hamdard Dawakhana* or *Hikmat* are growing side by side in an impressive way. Similarly, in China, Western and traditional Chinese medicine are coexisting and both are doing well. The Western medicine is being practiced in the big cities while in other smaller cities and the countryside, people have mostly access to the traditional medicine. This system is working very well in China.

In America, things are very different. Allopathic medicine continues to resist and downplay alternative medicine, but new drugs and new modalities of treatments suppress the older drugs and treatments, even when those are working well for many people. The public is finding on its own that alternative medicine sometimes works well for them. Yoga, meditation, acupressure and acupuncture, herbal medicine, chiropractic, *Ayurveda* and massage are becoming increasingly popular among Americans. However, mainstream medicine continues to frown upon them and continues to try to suppress them. The editor of JAMA (Journal of the American Medical Association) left his job when he devoted a whole issue to alternative medicine.

The linear approach also leads to a tendency towards compartmentalization. Instead of trying to understand the whole, we try to split philosophy or medicine into small parts. I have seen this tendency prevailing. For example, in medicine it sometimes becomes frustrating for the patient struggling to understand who is in charge of his health care. He could be seeing many physicians in different specialties but still lacks the satisfaction of knowing who his real doctor is.

Climate most likely played a role in the evolution of linear and multi-layered approaches just like it did in the evolution of cultivational and prescriptive spirituality. The climate was very mild in the Indian subcontinent. There was plenty of vegetation which grew year around. Survival was not a big problem. There was not cutthroat competition just to survive. The Western climate was much harsher. The growing season was much shorter. Survival was the main consideration. Competition for survival was intense. In a milder climate, tolerance for differences is more likely to develop. This tolerance leads to an environment conducive for dialogue. Tolerance and dialogue lead to a multi-layered approach.

In the harsher climate, people are less likely to have tolerance for different opinions. This leads to a linear approach. Whereas the harsher climate laid the foundation of the linear approach, capitalism further enhanced this tendency towards the linear approach. Capitalism promoted monopoly. Monopoly suppresses competition because the market has to expand at all cost. This is a question of survival. Just like the harsh climate, capitalism also pushes one to the lower centers. One can see the difference climate makes in thinking. We can see the difference between southern and northern Europe. Southern Europe, where the climate was mild, produced famous Greek scholars, but northern Europe produced Vikings.

Meat eating might have also played some role in the evolution of thought. Fats in the meat can reduce circulation to the brain, that reduces the release of endorphins. Endorphins keep a person calm. Low endorphin levels make people more aggressive. Calmness can lead to a multi-layered approach while aggression can lead to the linear approach.

A multi-layered approach leads to tolerance and coexistence which in turn promote concepts of pluralism and diversity. Pluralism and diversity are based on the principle that people are different yet they are equal. The linear approach, on the other hand, promotes a trend towards uniformity. Uniformity tries to negate differences and tries to dissolve the separate identities of different people. Diversity is natural while uniformity is unnatural. The linear approach can lead to confrontation with nature and can encourage the tendency to conquer nature. The multi-layered approach leads to the concept of harmony with nature. The question arises, can man conquer nature? Most certainly the answer is no. The best man can manage to do is live in harmony with nature. Wisdom lies in knowing and not testing the limits of one's power. Man is not powerful enough to conquer nature. Therefore, he must learn to live in harmony with nature. In the last two centuries, man has tried to conquer nature. Let us look at the results of this approach.

We have caused more environmental damage than any time before in history. More animal and plant species have disappeared in the last two centuries than in the millions of years before. Glaciers have receded all over the world. We went to Alaska last summer and saw how quickly the glaciers are receding. We were standing on dry ground where twenty years ago there was a glacier. It had receded more than half a mile. It is estimated that within this century all glaciers in India may completely melt. Ozone has been depleted from the atmosphere. This results in ultraviolet rays of the sun not being filtered because ozone was the natural filter for these rays. The ultraviolet rays are leading to a pandemic of skin cancer. Skin cancer is rising in Australia, Sweden, and the USA. There are estimates that in less than thirty years skin cancer will overtake heart disease and become the number one cause of death in America.

The environmental damage caused by over-utilization of natural resources has affected various regions in different ways. With global warming, the trapping of emission gases increases the greenhouse effect and has led to the melting of glaciers. This can lead to a rise in sea levels which threatens coastal areas. The inland regions have been effected by over-utilization of underground water, and as a result of this over-utilization, the water table of the underground water is constantly falling.

In our land in Punjab, I have seen the water table falling from 16 feet to 160 feet in about thirty years. This happened because of the so-called Green revolution in Punjab when Punjab's agricultural economy was integrated into the world market. In other words, it was globalized. Punjabi climate is semi-arid, which means there is less water to begin with. The *paddi* (rice) crop was brought to Punjab in a big way. It needs abundant water, which was taken from the ground leading to the fall of the water table. Punjab, which became the bread basket of India, is on the verge of becoming a desert unless some drastic measures are taken to reverse the trend of over-utilization of water.

The ground water is not the only victim of the linear approach of globalization. Globalization is the highest state of capitalist mode of production. Capitalism is based on the linear approach. There is only one consideration which matters, that is generating profit. How this will effect the environment and the effect on this generation of people and the social fabric are ignored. Again, Punjab is a typical example of how the switch from a multi-layered to a linear approach can have adverse effects. Punjab has a unique distinction in the field of spirituality and knowledge. The world's first book, *Rig Veda,* was written in Punjab and I believe the world's last major work in the field of spirituality and knowledge written there was, *Guru Granth Sahib,* the holy book of the Sikhs. In the last three decades, Punjab's main economy, the agrarian economy, became the only concern of Punjab. Generating more profit from agriculture became the only consideration. For a while it seemed to work. Punjab, with a land area of about 2% of India, was able to produce so much food that it was enough for the rest of India and there was so much surplus that there was no space available to store it. The social, cultural, and environmental impact were completely ignored. Cheap labor was brought from the other poorer states in India. An estimated two and a half million laborers migrated to Punjab. Punjabi peasants were idled. They decided to migrate to the Western countries in such a large number that was unheard of in Punjab.

This accelerated inward and outward migration into and out of Punjab completely destabilized the society. Congestion, pollution, slum culture, prostitution, drug addiction, AIDS, growing crime, violence, and falling educational standards are some of the consequences of the so-called green revolution. Punjab, the land which gave knowledge to the rest of the world now lags behind almost every other state in India in the field of education. Punjab is facing economic decline. It has already fallen from first to the fifth place and is still falling. Corruption is rampant. Social institutions have been destabilized and cultural values eroded. The institution of marriage has suffered the most. It has been commercialized and fake marriages for obtaining immigrant status in Western countries has become a very big problem for Punjab. The newly emerged capitalist farmer class, as a result of the so-called green revolution, completely betrayed the teachings of Guru Nanak on equality and universal brotherhood. They promoted chauvinistic and jingoistic values instead. Punjab is paying very dearly for switching from a traditional multi-layered approach to the linear approach of capitalism.

These problems are not limited to Punjab. The linear approach of globalization, which is limited to economic globalization alone, is adversely affecting the whole planet. Some areas, like Punjab, are affected more than others, but sooner or later, unless the present globalization is modified, every part of the world is destined to suffer a similar fate.

The linear approach of the present globalization has led to a unilateral policy by the United States which as a sole surviving superpower, sits at the top of the globalized empire created by this globalization. After the fall of the Soviet Union, America became the sole superpower of the world. No country could match the economic and military might of America. Nobody had the guts to question America, and nobody had the power to stop America. We can do whatever and wherever we want to do. This was a perfect set-up for the linear approach to be applied in the form of a unilateralist policy. Since nobody is strong enough to question us or stop us, then why should we bother to listen to what they have to say?

This unilateralist policy has actually led to growing American isolation. It is true that an average American still feels a sense of exaggerated national pride at the fact that there is nobody to match our power. However, the intellectually enlightened segment of America is showing growing concern over the results of the unilateralist policy and abandoning a multilateralistic approach. Sooner or later, the rest of America will have to wake up to what this approach has really done to the American interests. One can only hope that this awakening is not too late.

Let us examine the major events of the last decade to see if this unilateralist policy and abandoning multilateralilsm has led to growing American isolation or not. In 1991, during the first attack on Iraq (Desert Storm), America was able to get a mandate from the United Nations and had a broad alliance of countries representing almost all regions. Next came the attack on Yugoslavia. We were unable to get a mandate from the United Nations but were able to lineup NATO with us. Then came the terrorist attack of September 11, 2001. This attack reversed the trend of American isolation because a wave of sympathy started in the whole world. The invasion of Afghanistan after the terrorist attacks again had broad support. After that, we reverted to our unilateralist policy and abandoned the multilateralist consensus which was emerging. Then came the present attack on Iraq (May of 2003). We could neither get a mandate from the United Nations nor line up NATO. This war has further widened the gap between America and its traditional allies, Europe and Canada. Even in England, the only major European power to support us, anti-war sentiment is very widespread. England saw bigger antiwar protests and demonstrations against the Iraq war than any other event in recent history.

The linear approach leads to unilateralism which in turn promotes the concept of a unipolar world. The multi-layered approach, on the other hand, promotes multilateralism which leads to the concept of a multi-polar world. The question is which one of these two concepts is going to prevail. If we analyze the current events and trends, then it becomes obvious that the world is moving in the direction of multi-polarity. Can a policy which puts America against the current of history be a good thing for America? America's interests are best served by moving with the historical current and not against it. Moreover, America is a multicultural society which makes it more compatible with the concept of a multi-polar world. America has much more to gain by accepting the emerging world order of a multi-polar world than hanging on to a worn out idea of a unipolar world.

The linear and multi-layered approaches evolved as a result of geographical, historical, economic, and cultural factors. The means of transport and communication have led to a growing interaction between various regions and cultures. There is no reason to stick to a linear approach. We have to adopt good ideas no matter where they are coming from. This will expose us to the multi-layered approach which in turn will help us to develop a multilateralist policy. We cannot turn back the wheels of history. We cannot stop the change which is based on the currents of history. We have only two choices; we can either willingly accept the change, or we will be forced to accept it. It does not feel comfortable to be dragged by the change. To accept the change willingly will certainly be less painful. Even if we do not accept the fact that change is good for us, we can use the logic that the lesser of the two evils is better for us. Given the choices of accepting or resisting the change, accepting the change is certainly the lesser of the two evils. Guru Nanak's message can help us to accept the change because Guru Nanak preached that whatever is happening is happening because of the will of God, or we can say, because of the universal order. Therefore, accepting it is the best thing for us.

# CHAPTER THREE

## PERCEPTIVE, TRANSCENDENT, AND ULTIMATE REALITY

Reality has different levels. Generally, we limit our concept of reality by an understanding of reality as something we can feel with our sensations; we can experiment or reproduce it. This is also the scientific definition of reality, but this is the most basic form of reality, which we can call perceptive reality. Transcendent reality is the reality which is working behind visible reality, and ultimate reality is the source of all other realities.

Perceptive reality is not final reality because it is always changing. The factors which are working behind this visible reality and are responsible for the change can be called transcendent reality. The Eastern concept of reality is not uni-dimensional but is multidimensional. For example, for understanding reality we need knowledge. Knowledge is called *gian*. To understand different levels of reality, we also need different levels of knowledge. In other words, levels of knowledge correspond with levels of reality. Reality and knowledge are interwoven. Since perceptive reality is felt by our sensations, the level of knowledge that corresponds to that is called *indiyat gian,* which means sensory knowledge. *Indris* means sensations. *Budhigat gian* corresponds with transcendent reality. This means intellectual knowledge. *Budhi* (intellect) can transcend the visible reality. To reach ultimate reality, we need *Vastvik gian* (real knowledge). This level of knowledge can also be called *Tat gian* (essence of knowledge) or *Atmic gian* (spiritual knowledge).

We can also use terms such as information, knowledge, and wisdom to understand different levels of reality. Information corresponds to *Indrigat gian* and it is limited to perceptive reality. Knowledge corresponds to *Budhigat gian* and it helps us to understand transcendent reality. Wisdom, which rises above knowledge and can be considered *Vastvik gian* (real knowledge), is needed to understand ultimate reality.

After the industrial revolution, capitalism became the dominant mode of production. The church was still loyal to the old feudal order. The newly emerged capitalist class had two reasons to have unrealistic faith in science. The first, it felt it owed its very existence to science and the second, it wanted to undercut God and spirituality in order to undercut the power of the church. Therefore, it came up with scientific secularism. This secularism is a negative secularism because it is not based on respect for other's beliefs, but it has had a narrow connotation of suppressing the power of the church

Religion and spirituality were considered impediments to the unbridled growth of capitalism because they promoted values of moderation, austerity, humility, and restraint. These qualities prevent people from becoming good consumers. It appears that capitalism needed exactly the opposite values to be successful: extravagance, arrogance, selfishness, and greed, in order to make people better consumers. Therefore, from its inception, capitalism has tried to attack religion and spirituality under the pretext of promoting secularism. Capitalism used hypocrasy and double standards towards religion. In capitalist countries, capitalism cut the power of the church by insisting on separation between the state and the church. However, in the colonial countries, it lined up with Christianity to colonize other countries. The colonialists conquered other countries with a sword in one hand and a Bible in the other.

The present American ruling class is different than those earlier capitalists. I call it a techno-executive elite. This techno-executive elite has unrealistic expectations about its technology. The techno-executive elite seems to believe that its technology is superior to both man and God. It may feel it can maintain its control over America, and the whole world, with its technology.

The old capitalist class and the new techno-executive elite have either intentionally or unintentionally pitted science against spirituality. They have not understood the different levels of reality and they did not differentiate between information, knowledge, and wisdom. They feel since we have access to information, we will automatically become knowledgeable and wise. Information has to be assimilated before it becomes knowledge, and knowledge has to be practiced before it becomes wisdom. They also do not seem to understand that science only deals with perceptive reality. Science increases the reach of our senses but it cannot transcend them. For example, a microscope can magnify objects and see much smaller things than a naked eye. Similarly, a telescope can see much farther than we can see with a naked eye. Still, there are always limits of scientific reach. In the final analysis, science deals with finite knowledge and spirituality deals with infinite knowledge.

If we understand the concepts of perceptive, transcendent, and ultimate realities, then we will realize that there is no conflict between science and spirituality. One deals with the finite and the other deals with infinite knowledge. We can even go one step further and say that they can be mutually complementary. The fusion of Western capitalism and Eastern spirituality can be beneficial for the whole of mankind. The modern tendency of compartmentalizing and fragmenting knowledge has helped make science and spirituality adversaries. In the Eastern tradition, there was never a conflict between science and spirituality. Scientists were spiritual people and sages and saints made scientific discoveries.

We can also see the fusion of science and spirituality in health care. In almost every culture, spirituality was an integral part of health care. In the Indian subcontinent, health care, *Ayurveda,* was made a part of *Vedas (vedang).* The *Vedas* were considered *aprush* (not created by a human being, in other words, the word of God). In China, acupuncture is based on the flow of *chi* (life energy). which was called *prana* in India. All these concepts were developed by spiritual people. In ancient Greece, spirituality was an integral part of health care. Jesus and many Christian saints practiced a healing art. In the Islamic tradition, *hikmat* and *hakim,* words for health care and health care provider, have spiritual connotations. In native America, the medicine man was a health care provider and a spiritual leader. Even in modern medicine we can find symbols for evoking spiritual power. When we write a prescription, we evoke power of the ancient Egyptian god Horus. The serpent (caduceus) is very widely used by medical institutions, including the American Medical Association and the American College of Surgeons. This is a continuation of the ancient traditional symbol of kundalini (serpent).

Marxist countries and the consumerist capitalist class have tried to divorce spirituality from science. Already we are seeing a trend of spiritual revival. Many medical schools in America have introduced spirituality as a part of the curriculum. There is a growing acceptance by people of the spiritual aspect of medicine. The *Readers Digest* of January 2004 has quoted a *Newsweek* magazine poll to show that seventy-two percent of Americans would like their doctors to discuss spirituality. Yoga, meditation, acupuncture, and tai chi are being used by growing numbers of Americans to improve and maintain their health. Vegetarianism is also finding more adherents. Many restaurants and fast food chains like McDonalds and Burger King have also introduced vegetarian dishes in their menus.

Let us look at some examples so that we can understand differences between perceptive, transcendent, and ultimate reality. If we look at a child and an adult, then we can see that the adult is stronger than the child. This is perceptive reality. If we try to understand the forces working behind this visible reality then we can understand that the child is growing and the adult has already achieved his maximum growth potential. Therefore, the adult is declining (in strength). We can conclude, based on transcendent reality, that one day the child will be stronger than the adult. The ultimate reality is that neither the child nor the adult is going to live forever. All organisms which are born will die. People continue to be born and die. We can also conclude that birth, maintenance, and death are a continuous phenomenon which can be called constant creation. If there is constant creation then there has to be a constant creator. This constant creator has been called Eternal Truth or ultimate reality by Guru Nanak. Guru Nanak says that the Eternal truth manifests itself by three continuous phenomena of creation, maintenance, and death. These three tasks are assigned to three different gods, Brahma, Vishnu, and Mahesh (Shiva). Brahma is in charge of creation, Vishnu is in charge of maintenance, and Shiva is in charge of death. These three gods have been assigned specific tasks by the continuous creator who is beyond them. That is why the creator is called *parbrahm* which means beyond Brahm. The creator is also called *Paramatma* (supreme Soul). Guru Nanak says that there is only one continuous creator *(Karta Purkh);* He is *Akalmoorat* (timeless), *Nirankar* (formless), *Ajoni* (unborn, beyond death), and *Saibhang* (He creates Himself). Guru Nanak says that there is the eternal truth *(Hai bhi sach Hosi ach),* which is ultimate reality. Guru Nanak says that there is only one eternal truth since everything was created from the same reality and everything will merge into the same reality. This concept of ultimate reality lays the foundation of Guru Nanak's philosophy of the unity of mankind.

Since all men are created from the same source, then how can it be that some are good and some are bad? How can it be that some are superior and some are inferior when they all happen to be children of the same father? Besides the unity of mankind, this philosophy also lays the foundation for accepting principles of love, tolerance, peaceful coexistence, pluralism, diversity, universal concern, and universal well-being. Guru Nanaak says that if anybody believes that there is more than one ultimate reality, then they are ignorant or have delusions. Guru Nanak condemned dualism and parallelism, which alleges there is more than one ultimate reality.

Let us try to apply the concept of perceptive, transcendent, and ultimate reality to the current global situation. According to the visible (perceptive) reality we have a Western dominated, uni-polar world. America is the most powerful country. Christianity is the largest religion. If we try to analyze the forces working behind these visible realities (transcendent reality), then we may come to a different conclusion. Asia may become the leading region, China the most powerful country, and Islam the largest religion in the 21$^{st}$ century. If we try to understand the ultimate reality, then we will come to the conclusion that ultimately whatever is happening is happening by the will of God, or is part of the universal order. There are different countries, nations, races, colors, religions, and cultural groups, but they are all manifestations of the same ultimate reality. The feeling of other-ness is the product of our ignorance and delusion. If we transcend the visible reality and try to understand the ultimate reality, then we will become aware of the fact that we are all part of the whole. If we do not see God in all then we have not really understood God. The fact is that we are all inter-related, including people, other living organisms, and non-living objects. This concept of a global community is what Guru Nank calls *Sarbat* (all inclusive community).

We should also try to understand the relationship of humility and arrogance with knowledge. Knowledge leads to humility and arrogance is a product of ignorance. If we try to understand concepts of perceptive, transcendent, and ultimate reality, then we will become humble because reality is so vast and complex. We may realize how little we know compared to what can be known. On the other hand, if we do not understand these concepts, we have a tendency to become arrogant because of our ignorance. We feel that we understand everything but this feeling is based upon knowing a very small part of the total reality.

In the modern so-called scientific age we have put all our faith in science and technology. We are ignoring a simple fact that science only deals with perceptive reality. Perceptive reality is the lowest level of reality. Just like we do not understand the fact that information is the lowest level of our journey towards wisdom. In both cases, confusing preliminary and the lowest level with the final and the highest level, points to our ignorance. The fact remains that science is limited, it can extend its limits by more scientific discoveries, but it will never be able to transcend limits. Scientific knowledge will remain finite whereas the ultimate reality is infinite. Guru Nanak says that the Eternal Truth (ultimate reality) is infinite and cannot be comprehended in the realms of physical, mental, and intellectual existence. To understand the ultimate reality we have to transcend our physical, mental, and intellectual existence *(shareer, man,* and *budhi)* and reach a level of spiritual awareness where we recognize our true self, the essence of our existence *(mool tat).* Then we become aware that we come from the ultimate reality and we will merge into the same reality.

Many of the problems we are facing now are products of our ignorance. Guru Nanak says that our ignorance is the cause of our pain and suffering. These problems arise because we have unrealistic expectations of our scientific knowledge and technological capabilities. With our technological progress, we have been able to gather far more information than at any other time in the history of mankind. However, we do not seem to understand that all the information, all our scientific knowledge, and all our technological progress has not necessarily made us any wiser than other people who lived before us. Actually, our arrogance might have made us more ignorant. The people before us probably did not have so many unrealistic expectations as we have. Trying to understand the concepts of perceptive, transcendent, and ultimate reality may help us with the problem of arrogance. This may also help to change the confrontational relationship between science and spirituality. Becoming knowledgeable of these concepts may also help us to become more tolerant of each other and take the first step towards the concept of a global community.

# CHAPTER FOUR

## COLONIALISM, IMPERIALISM, AND GLOBALIZATION

The words colonialism and imperialism have existed since ancient times but the word globalization is relatively a new phenomenon. Ancient Rome had colonies in Europe, the Middle East, and Africa. Egypt, Assyria, Babylonia, and Persia established large empires in ancient times. The term imperial army has been used for the Roman army. However, I want to use colonialism and imperialism in the modern sense, that is, in relation to capitalist mode of production. These terms were first used in the modern sense by leftist intellectuals, but now they are getting wide acceptance. The version of modern history based on these concepts is generally accepted by the leftists. However, it may not be universally accepted. After the renaissance, in the fifteenth century, many European countries built their industrial bases. With advancements in science and technology, as well because of the emerging capitalist mode of production, industrial output increased greatly.

There was intense competition between the different European countries to seek new territories to obtain raw material for their industries as well as markets for their finished products. Production had already exceeded the needs of their own countries. This is the beginning of colonialism. From the fifteenth century up to the nineteenth century, this period can be called the era of colonialism. From the nineteenth century to the later part of the twentieth century, it can be considered the era of imperialism. This era can also be called the era of neocolonialism. The later part of the twentieth century and up to the present, it can be called the age of globalization.

Colonialism, imperialism, and globalization are not separate and independent phenomena but are different stages in development of the capitalist mode of production. That is why the divisions between them are not watertight and there is a lot of overlapping. For example, the phenomenon of globalization started with colonization and continues through the period of imperialism. However, each one of these phenomena has certain distinctive features. Roughly speaking, capitalism can be divided into crude capitalism and relatively refined capitalism. Colonialism was the period of crude capitalism whereas imperialism and globalization can be considered periods of the gradual refinement of capitalism.

In colonialism, brute force was used to conquer other countries and nations. There was physical occupation. The foreign power sent its armies and officials to rule the other people's land. The rulers and the ruled generally belonged to different ethnic groups. The rulers had more advanced technologies than the people they ruled. The major colonial powers were England, France, Spain, Holland, and Portugal. England was the largest colonial power. It boasted that the sun never sets on the British empire. England had the largest industrial production in the world. At the end of the nineteenth century, England was producing more than the rest of the world combined. Capitalism was most developed in England.

In the fourteenth and fifteenth centuries, there was glamour associated with anything connected to India. Indian spices were considered exotic in Europe. Even in the Byzantine Empire (now Turkey) the word Hind, meaning Indian, was a symbol of prestige and status. In the early fifteenth century Portugal and Spain began to send explorers in search of sea routes to India. At that time land routes were controlled by the Muslims. Therefore, they controlled trade between Asia and Europe. The European colonialists had to bypass the land routes and look to the sea for an alternate route. In an effort to reach India and the Far East, the Americas were discovered.

During the seventeenth century the Dutch and the English took control of Asian trade from the Portuguese. The Dutch took control of many islands in southeast Asia and called them Dutch East Indies (now Indonesia). The English established the East India Company and became strong in India. Eventually the East India Company became the ruler of all India. India became the most prized possession of the British empire, often called "jewel in the crown." The French, Dutch, and Portuguese were marginalized by the English. The French fought fierce battles with the English for control of India but they lost. The French were left with a very small colony on the Southeast coast of India called Pondicherry. The Portuguese were left with another tiny territory on the West coast of India called Goa. Controlling India gave England prestige and power unparalleled by any other colonial power. Out of all the British colonies, India was the most developed socially, politically, and economically. Before being colonized, India was already a big and strong empire. According to European visitors, India in the sixteenth century was as powerful as England of that time. India also provided a trained work force and had a well-educated middle class which was recruited by the English to create a bureaucratic elite in India and used to run other colonies along with the skilled Indian work force. The Indians were used both as skilled laborers as well as mid-executives by the English in many countries, particularly in South East Asian countries (Malaysia and Singapore), China, and Africa. The English edged out the other colonialists in Canada and America just like they did in India. Again, the main rivals were the French who fought four wars with the British from 1689 to 1763. After the last war, which the British won, they took over almost all of the French colonial possessions in North America.

By the early nineteenth century, England had established itself as the leading power of the world. It even added Australia to its prized possessions. The Euro-centric world which had emerged after colonialism now started to become uni-polar with Great Britain as the supreme power.

In the era of colonialism, brute force was used to achieve its objectives. Armies were sent to conquer and occupy other lands and gain control over the natural resources of the lands. The indigenous industry was forcibly suppressed. Christianity was sometimes forced on people even if they had their own religions. In some cases, superiority of the European race over other races was openly asserted. Some parks in India had signs which read, "Indians and dogs not allowed."

Having been born and raised in Punjab, India, I have heard a lot about the cruelty and oppression of colonialists. When the British conquered India, very fine cloth was being made in India. The British wanted to sell the cloth made in their factories in England. There are tales that the British chopped off the hands of the workers who were making fine clothing material. There are also stories about the English urinating on and kicking the sacred Hindu gods. There are other stories which can be historically authenticated. For example, Maharaja Dalip Singh, son of Maharaja Ranjit Singh, was forcibly converted to Christianity at the age of seven over the strong objections of his mother, Maharani Jind Kaur. Similarly, after the fall of the Sikh empire in Punjab, a Sikh was converted to Christianity in Amritsar (the holy city of the Sikhs) and his hair was shorn in front of the Golden Temple, the holiest place for Sikhs, to humiliate the Sikhs.

Another example of colonialist cruelty, also in the nineteenth century, can be cited in Delhi, in 1857, when Bahadur Shah Zafar, the last Mogul ruler of India lost the war against the British forces. He was hiding in the tomb of Hamayu, his forefather, when the British general came to meet him there. He said he had brought gifts for him. These were platters covered with fine clothes. When the emperor took the clothes off he found heads of his two sons who were beheaded by the British.

Still another example of the nineteenth century cruelty of colonialists can be given from the Chinese history. The Chinese authorities were trying to control opium smuggling in China. One time they caught a Chinese boat which was using a British flag and was trying to smuggle opium. When the British governor in Hong Kong heard about this incident, he became furious. He asked how the Chinese dared to stop a boat which was carrying a British flag, even if it was not British. He ordered the British navy to teach the Chinese a lesson. The British gun boats pounded Canton and killed twenty thousand Chinese. The Chinese have re-written history of two centuries of the colonialist period and have brought out all the atrocities and crimes committed against their people by the colonialists. This includes the crimes of the Christian priests who engaged in spreading drugs and raping and sexually abusing the Chinese children.

India, which is still ruled by the Westernized elite, has bent backward to suppress the horrible history of the British colonial era. India has the rare distinction of making a British colonial ruler as the first head of state of independent India. Indians also made history when some of them came to see off the British who were leaving India in 1947, when India became independent. Some of these people were crying and sobbing. The situation in India is finally changing, Indian rulers who felt more comfortable in dealing with the Western countries than their Asian counterparts are now showing a tilt towards Asia and the East.

The open and brutal use of force by colonialists alienated many people and resistance movements emerged in many parts of the world. It became almost impossible for the colonialists to maintain physical control over their colonies. This situation led to a change in tactics by the colonialists to maintain their control without being physically present all the time. This phenomenon can be called neo-colonialism or imperialism. Instead of using physical force, the imperialists used the force of capital. The industrial and finance capital (banking) merged, leading to powerful multi-national corporations. Instead of sending marching armies, a section of the capitalists in the developing countries and a section of ruling bureaucrats replaced the colonial armies. This class was more efficient then the old colonial armies because they were of the same race, same color, and same religion. There was less resistance to their rule than the rule of colonialists. Lenin called imperialism the highest stage of capitalism. He did not know his own country and his own party would become one of the leading imperialist powers in the world. The Soviet social imperialism was more deceptive and aggressive than the traditional Western imperialism because it was outwardly socialist and it was based on centralized bureaucracy, the so-called Communist Party, which exerted far more control than the traditional Western multi-national corporations.

The rise of Soviet social imperialism changed the uni-polar imperialist world, divided into areas of influence of two superpowers, the United States and the Soviet Union. Imperialism also received resistance from national liberation struggles. The struggle in Vietnam weakened the United States and the national liberation struggle in Afghanistan weakened the Soviet Union to a point that it collapsed.

After the collapse of the Soviet Union, there remained only one superpower and the world reverted to a uni-polar one. Uni-polar world has meant Anglo-American domination. In the era of earlier uni-polar imperialism, the British imperialism was the leading imperialist power. Some forces in the United States want to continue the uni-polar policy of Great Britain. But after the fall of the Soviet Union, the world has moved to an era of globalization with the United States at the top of this new world order. Globalization can be defined as the highest stage of imperialism.

How does globalization differ from imperialism? In imperialism, power of the capital was the major instrument of projecting power. In globalization, technology and culture are used along with capital, for domination. Colonialism was physical domination, imperialism was financial domination and globalization is complete domination.

In the old era British imperialist domination, the domination was not over the whole world. There were areas still not under British influence. Moreover, people under British rule still retained their cultures. The British never talked about dissolving national borders. In the new age of globalization, means of communication and transportation have developed to a degree that the whole world has become one unit. Some people are saying that national borders have become irrelevant. The whole world has been transformed into one big market. The consumerist culture has become the dominant culture and the other cultures are feeling suppressed.

The only thing this globalization has been able to achieve is integration of markets. We can call this economic globalization only. There has been no integration of different cultures where good values from the different cultures could have been integrated. Similarly, this globalization wants to integrate people either as consumers or as producers, but not as human beings. The concept of globalization is based entirely on expanding markets and increasing profits without any concern for its social impact.

This purely mechanical approach of globalization and the fact that it has eroded peoples' culture and values has led to two devastating effects. First, there is increased polarization between rich and poor countries and between the rich and the poor inside them. The second effect is that it has legitimized making money by any means. This phenomenon has led to an increase in corruption. The bureaucracy which evolved in the colonies and neo-colonies was always corrupt, but corruption has reached new heights after globalization. Everybody wants to make a fast buck and get rich quickly. Some of the social benefits for the working people and others have been withdrawn under globalization. The result of this cutback has been very detrimental to education and healthcare for the poor. In India, I have seen healthcare and education for the poor, which was already marginal, go from bad to worse.

Globalization has also led to uneven and unplanned development of big cities in the developing countries. Infrastructure of the cities, such as roads, sewage, and water supplies are in terrible shape, resulting in ghettos, "Ghettoization," slum culture, congestion, and filth in many big cities of the developing countries. Needless to say, the environment has taken a very big beating. The quality of air and water has deteriorated considerably.

Even though changes brought by globalization have hurt the developing countries more than the developed countries, yet the developed countries have been unable to escape the ill effects of globalization. Polarization and the gap between the rich and poor continues to widen. The middle class, which provided social stability, is being constantly eroded. A small section is joining the rich while a large section is joining the ranks of the poor. Education and healthcare have been adversely affected. Access to quality healthcare and good education is becoming more difficult for the people coming from the lower strata of society. It is equally difficust to jump and overcome the prosperity gap.

A quick overview of colonialism, imperialism, and globalization has shown us that both capitalism and Marxism have been unable to come up with a global perspective which could have helped to make life better for the majority of people on the planet. In spite of scientific and technological advancements, quality of life for a vast majority of people has not improved. Neither the old crude capitalism nor the new liberal capitalism has been able to acquire a humanitarian perspective. The Soviet Union and the European countries had a chance to prove that Marxism can do a better job than capitalism as far as making life better for the majority of people is concerned, but they blew their chance. Both were unable to develop a global perspective. The reason they could not develop a global perspective was that for all practical purposes, they denied the spiritual aspect of life. Without having a spiritual aspect, we cannot cultivate values such as tolerance, love, peaceful coexistence, universal concern, and a universal welfare. These values are the missing element in both of these philosophies. These values are also the essence of Guru Nanak's message. We have to give spirituality a chance before things turn from bad to worse for most of us.

# CHAPTER FIVE

## CAPITALISM AND MARXISM

Capitalism and Marxism are the two major philosophies of the modern age. I feel they are like cousins. Capitalism is based on the principle of generating profit; in Marxist terminology, this is called surplus value. Capitalism believes that market forces of supply and demand regulate the economy and are able to exert a sort of self control. Free market policy also includes free competition. In practice, in unadulterated capitalism, this means survival of the fittest. Those enterprises that could not compete had to perish, and in the pure capitalism, one who does not work will not eat. Capitalist philosophy is based on the belief that competition is healthy and helps enterprises stay productive and profitable.

Marxism arose as a counter philosophy to what it perceived as the dehumanizing philosophy of capitalism. Marxism was based on the principle that labor creates value. The proletariat or the working class creates surplus value which is appropriated by the capitalist class in the name of profit. Marxism believed that free markets, free competition, and democracy are a sham. Instead of freedom and democracy, there is a dictatorship of the bourgeoisie. Marxism was based on the principle that class struggle is the motivating force which brings change in society and in a class society, the state power is usurped by one class and it suppresses other classes. Marxism also believed that with the growth of capitalism, the capitalist class causes conditions for its own demise, strengthening the proletariat by creating conditions for their better organization. Therefore, proletarian revolution was most likely to occur in the most developed capitalist society. The early Marxists like Marx and Engels were revolutionary humanists.

Neither capitalism nor Marxism have survived in their original forms. Both have changed. Both have influenced each other and led to modifications of the other. Capitalism changed from its original cut and dried state and instead of absolute free competition and free market rules, we had controls and intervention by the state to regulate profit and competition. Workman's compensation, welfare, tariffs, and subsidiary grants are few examples of intervention by the state on behalf of collective interests of society.

Marxism was, similarly, modified by the influence of capitalism. Gradually, Marxism lost its revolutionary humanism and became mostly "economism." Things did not turn the way Marxism had predicted. For example, according to Marxism, proletarian revolution should have come in the most developed capitalist society, that was England at that time. Instead, it was the most backward capitalism in Europe (Russia) which saw the first proletarian revolution. As Marxism lost its revolutionary zeal and capitalism adopted many social welfare concepts, the difference between the two kept narrowing. In the end, traditional Marxism in practice became a centralized bureaucratic capitalistic state as opposed to relatively free monopoly capitalism of the traditional capitalist countries. In the traditional capitalist countries, various capitalist corporations shared the state power and resources whereas in traditional Marxist countries the state power and resources were monopolized by the centralized bureaucracy.

Capitalism and Marxism tried to demonize one another. Capitalist countries called themselves free societies but called Marxist countries an iron curtain.

Marxists and communists were portrayed as heartless and cruel heathens. Senator McCarthy's crusade against communists was like the Spanish inquisition. Marxists painted an equally derogatory picture of capitalists, calling them exploiters and blood suckers of the people. This propaganda was quite effective.

The words colonialism, capitalism, and imperialism were seen as having negative connotations. Both capitalism and Marxism shared some basic concepts. Both were Western philosophies, both shared the belief that economic transformation of society was more important than changing human beings. After the fall of the Soviet Union, the Western capitalists started beating their chest in a lap of victory. They had won the cold war; Marxism was dead, and capitalism had emerged victorious. Even the words capitalism and imperialism, which were never used by the capitalist countries before, found new acceptance and even a degree of respect. The victorious and rejuvenated capitalists embarked upon a new voyage to globalization with great enthusiasm. The whole world was going to become one large market. Making profit and earning money had a new degree of respect never seen before. It felt that the triumph of capitalism was final and there was no chance of change in the near future.

All this euphoria did not last very long. Marxism seems to be making a comeback in the form of the anti-globalization movement. In Europe, in South America, and even in the United States, anti-globalization forces started getting organized and came under the leadership of leftist intellectuals inspired by Marxism. Opposition to the policies of globalization became a rallying point for all the forces opposed to the traditional capitalism. The world had never seen such massive anti-globalization protests at gatherings of WTO and IMF. Many South American countries saw leftist and Marxist leaders voted to power. These countries include Venezuela, Argentina, and Brazil. Socialists were voted to power in Spain. In a recent election in India, Marxists won more seats than in any other election in the history of independent India.

Then came the war in Iraq. This gave another impetus to the revival of the leftist movement. This looked like a déjà vu of anti-

Vietnam war protests. Even England, a country which was supporting the war, saw the largest anti-war demonstration in its history. America is experiencing the phenomenon of intellectual polarization. Among the general population, there is a rightward shift but in the intellectual and academic circles, a leftward shift seems to be the trend. War is still popular with the general public, but among intellectuals and academicians, anti-war sentiment prevails.

There is another peculiar phenomenon which has become noticeable in America, particularly after the September 11 terrorist attack. There is religious and spiritual revival. However, the religious revival and the spiritual revival are neither parallel nor similar. They seem to be moving in opposite directions. The religious revival forces are shifting to the right. They are pro Bush, pro globalization ,and pro war. They have close links with the big corporations. They are less tolerant of minorities and view multiculturalism negatively. The spiritual revival movement is moving exactly in the opposite direction. They are leaning to the left, they are generally against Bush, against war and are generally opposed to globalization. They are more tolerant of minorities. They view multiculturalism favorably. The spiritual revivalists have a positive feeling towards Eastern spirituality.

The religion revivalists in America are out of step with the other Western countries. In Europe and South America, Christianity and Marxism are finding a common enemy—globalization. Another reason that the religious right in America cannot have a global following is that Islam, the fastest growing major religion of the world, is taking a strong anti-globalization stand. Therefore, the rise of the religious right in America will continue pushing the country into unilateralism and isolationism.

The war in Iraq compelled America to seek support from the United Nations. Already the aggressive persistence of the teach-them-a-lesson approach is losing some of its steam. For the time being, we seem to have put on hold our policies of going after other *rogue states* like North Korea and Iran. Even with Libya, a relatively conciliatory approach is being applied.

The degeneration of traditional Marxism into centralized bureaucratic capitalism was made more complicated by another element—the Russian chauvinism. This led to the emergence of Soviet social imperialism. The communist party was itself transformed into a centralized bureaucratic class. This elitist class not only suppressed its own people, but started suppressing other nations and countries. Russia's relations with the east European countries were not based upon proletarian internationalism. Soviet invasions of Hungary, Czechoslovakia, and Afghanistan are a few examples of Soviet social imperialism.

This policy of the Soviet Union was resented by many people all over the world. This policy also resulted in the re-emergence of the rightist forces in the West. Those forces had been marginalized after the Vietnam War. Leaders like Ronald Reagan and Margaret Thatcher emerged in the West. These leaders labeled the Soviet Union *the evil empire*. Finally, the Soviet Union collapsed and the West won the cold war. The traditional capitalism, which can be called consumer capitalism, was gradually being modified to utilitarian capitalism, which is responsive to humanitarian and social concerns. With resurgence of the right, this trend was reversed and consumerist capitalism again became the dominant type of capitalism, especially in the United States.

After the fall of the Soviet Union, traditional Marxists were demoralized all over the world. The United States emerged as the sole superpower and the central and leading force of globalization. After the initial euphoria about globalization, it became clear to many people in the world that globalization was not any new phenomenon but was the reemergence of the old consumerist capitalism. This could be called an old wine in a new bottle. Globalization quickly became unpopular and opposition to the policies of globalization started growing and became very widespread. In Europe and in other countries, the trend started changing. One after the other, the right leaning leaders were replaced by the left leaning leaders. But in the United States, the rightward shift continued. Both Republican and Democratic parties continued their march to the right.

This rightward march in America is at odds with other countries including its allies. America's relations with Europe and even Canada became more strained and America's differences with the United

Nations also started widening. This phenomenon led to a vicious cycle; the more other countries resisted and opposed America, the more America moved to the right. This was due to two reasons, one was the feeling of retaliation and the other was that America enjoyed the role of the only superpower in the world and could do anything anywhere. Nobody had the right or power to question America. The growing American isolation reached its peak when it decided to invade Iraq without the support of United Nations or NATO.

After a quick victory in Iraq, it became painfully obvious that winning a war is easy but winning peace can prove very difficult. The longer the war drags on in Iraq, the greater the chances of this conflict becoming like the Vietnam war. This can increase polarization in America; either the rightward trend will be reversed, or the country will move to the extreme right. How it will effect America remains to be seen, but already, along with anti-globalization sentiment, this is creating favorable conditions for revival of Marxism worldwide.

Marxism today is different than the original Marxism whose principles were laid down by Karl Marx in *Das Kapital* and the *Communist Manifesto*. Marx saw class struggle inside a country as the primary impetus for social and political change. He saw the struggle between the bourgeoisie (capitalist class) and the working class (proletariat) as the main struggle. His theory was that as capitalism develops, it will strengthen the proletariat. The mass scale production will bring the proletariat together and also help them to organize better. Eventually, they will become so strong that they will overthrow the capitalist class and establish dictatorship of the proletariat which will then develop into socialism. Everybody will work according to their capacity and will be paid according to their work. There will be no exploitation of one class by the other. Means of production will be collectively owned by society. The differences in people's earnings will still remain because they will be paid according to their work, not according to their needs. Therefore, the state will still be needed. Communism was a utopia where people will become so tolerant and sensitive to other peoples' needs that they will be ready to follow the principle, "from each according to their capacity, to each according to their needs." In other words, one will work according to one's capacity, but will be paid according to his needs. For example, if one is single he will be paid less than the other person who has a family even though they did the same work.

It soon became obvious that things did not happen according to Marx's formulations. According to Marx, proletarian revolution was most likely to come in England, which was the most developed capitalist society. Instead, revolution came in Russia which was the most backward capitalist country in Europe, often called the sick man of Europe. Lenin tried to explain these discrepancies. His writings, *State and Revolution* and *Imperialism, the Highest Stage of Capitalism* tried to explain these new developments. He explained that capitalism had transformed into imperialism where the finance capital and industrial capital merged. Capitalists were no longer confined to the national boundaries, but with their finance capital, they could control other countries. This led to super profits with which they were able to give more concessions to their own working class and thereby avoid confrontation inside the capitalist countries, between the capitalist class and the proletariat. Instead of the class contradiction between the imperialist countries, the contradiction between the imperialist countries and the nations which were subjected to their control became the main contradiction. As for why revolution came in Russia, he tried to explain this phenomenon by the role played by the communist party. He said that if the communist party, the vanguard of the proletariat, becomes organized in a country, then it can become the major factor in bringing revolution.

After Lenin, when Stalin came to power, other problems in Marxism became apparent. The main problem was the national question. Marxism had tried to give the impression that after resolving class contradiction, the national question will be automatically resolved.

The tendency of Russian chauvinism and resentment in the other nations in the Soviet Union was becoming apparent at the time of Stalin. Stalin tried to address these issues in his book *Marxism and the National Question*. It was too little and too late. Moreover, Stalin suppressed inner democracy inside the communist party. Many Marxists were disillusioned with Marxism. A typical example can be given of the famous Indian Marxist M.N. Roy. Lenin had great regard for him and Roy played a very prominent role in the communist international movement. Later on, he abandoned Marxism and came up with his theory of Radical Humanism. He did not find much following among the Indian Marxists and was isolated. His American-born wife continued to propagate his radical humanist philosophy in India, but she was also suppressed.

After Stalin, the traditional Marxism could not produce a leader of international stature. It was Mao Tse-tung, the leader of the most populous country, China, who became the leading Marxist in the world. Marxism should today be appropriately called Marxism-Leninism-Mao Tse-tung thought. It has become apparent that while capitalism still remains a Western philosophy, its cousin, Marxism, has been "Easternized." Mao Tse-tung can be considered more of an Eastern philosopher rather than a traditional Marxist. Born in a peasant family, Mao Tse-tung was an ardent Chinese nationalist. He was at odds with Stalin and the traditional Marxists from the very beginning, but his differences with the Soviet Union grew to a point that towards the later part of his life, he started considering Soviet Union as the main enemy of China and advocated a tactical alliance with the United States to check the growing power of the Soviet social imperialism.

Deep in his heart, Mao Tse-tung believed in the superiority of the East. He used terms as East is red and eastern wind is always stronger than western wind. Mao's primary appeal to the Chinese was to restore China's status and prestige in the world and to undo injustice, humiliation, and the atrocities committed against China by Western powers. China was forced to sign unequal and humiliating treaties by the Western powers. Mao Tse-tung deeply studied four thousand years of Chinese history.

He tried to modify Marxism to the Chinese concrete conditions. Mao Tse-tung developed new concepts in Marxism; the three most important ones are: theories of new democratic revolution, on contradictions, and on peoples' war. His theory of new democratic revolution was a big break from the traditional Marxism. Traditional Marxism held on to the view that in order to have a proletarian revolution, there must be a capitalist development moving the society from a feudal and colonial society. Mao Tse-tung expounded the theory that imperialism has changed the traditional feudal and colonial societies and they should be more appropriately called semi-feudal and semi-colonial societies. He said that in these societies, we can bypass the development to a capitalist society by the new democratic revolution which can directly lead to a proletarian revolution. He advocated an alliance of four classes: proletariat, peasantry, petit bourgeoisie, and nationalist bourgeoisie against the three adversaries of imperialism, feudalism, and bureaucratic capitalism

The nationalist capitalists wanted the national market for their products. Generally, these were smaller capitalists. The bigger capitalists aligned themselves with imperialists and wanted to sell products made in imperialistic countries or products made in their own countries in collaboration with imperialists.

The Marxist theory is based on Hegel's theory of dialectic and is called dialectical materialism. The second law of dialectic says that there is unity of the opposites. Mao Tse-tung expanded and clarified this law into his theory of contradictions. He studied contradictions from various aspects and based his strategy on the analysis of contradictions. He divided contradictions into principle and secondary, antagonistic and non-antagonistic, and he stressed universality (generality) and peculiarity of a contradiction. The principle contradiction is that contradiction on whose resolution depends resolution of other (secondary) contradictions. Antagonistic contradictions are between enemies and friends and have to be resolved with force (violence), but non-antagonistic contradictions are among friends and can be resolved peacefully. By accepting the universality and peculiarity of a contradiction, Mao Tse-tung comes close to accepting the Eastern spiritual concept of *Brahm* (macrocosm) and *Jeev* (microcosm) or *Paratma* (supreme soul) and *Jeevatma* (individual soul).

Mao Tse-tung might have taken one step farther and related the second law of dialectic (contradiction) to the third law, which is the law of negation. In other words, a new thing emerges from the old in integrating two aspects. Resolution of a contradiction according to Mao will lead to emergence of new contradictions—contradictions are always going to be there. This is where Marxism, including Maoism, has failed to grasp the concept of ultimate reality. They have limited themselves to perceptive and transcendental reality only. Guru Nanak says that *Homay* (your false identity) is responsible for parallelism and dualism. If you are able to dissolve your false identity, then you merge with the eternal truth (ultimate reality). Then you are in a perfect state of harmony and equipoise because there will be no contradiction in that state. If a drop merges with the ocean, then water of the drop cannot be separated from the water of the ocean. This is a stage of absolute unity.

Marxism, including Maoism, does not have a concept of absolute unity. Unity will always be relative to a Marxist. Even in the utopia of communism, only class contradictions will be resolved. New contradictions will emerge. Therefore, even in the Marxist utopia, there is no hope for perfect harmony.

Still, in another way, Mao Tse-tung came close to accepting concepts of Eastern spirituality, but again fell short of accepting it. This is his theory of cultural revolution. The traditional Marxism did not accept culture as an independent entity. The traditional Marxism was of the view that economics is the infrastructure on which all other bourgeoisie institutions, including political, social and cultural are built. These are called superstructure. These institutions are only built to protect the economic interests of the ruling bourgeoisie (capitalist class). Therefore, revolution has to be in the field of economics, snatching the means of production from the bourgeoisie and bringing them under the control of the proletariat. Once the infrastructure is captured, the superstructure will automatically change. Clearly, Mao's theory of cultural revolution is a deviation from traditional Marxism. Mao sees a possibility of superstructure effecting infrastructure; in other words, superstructure can be an independent entity. This postulation attacks the very essence of Marxism, materialism, and by Marxist standards, can be called idealism, to which materialism is in constant opposition. If, instead of the cultural revolution Mao, had incorporated the concept of spiritual revolution, then he would have accepted Eastern philosophy.

Mao talked about a series of cultural revolutions, but the very first cultural revolution led to so much turmoil that extremes were committed. If we use Mao's terminology, then non-antagonistic contradictions were treated like antagonistic contradictions. There was no room for tolerating any kind of difference, no room for dialogue. Guru Nanak emphasized the principle of dialogue to resolve differences. Even while Mao was alive, cultural revolution had to be withdrawn. After Mao's death, it appears that Chinese Marxists have moved closer to traditional Marxism. They are concentrating all these efforts for the economic development of China and raising the living standard of people. Apparently, China is making great progress in economic, scientific, and technological fields, but in the field of ideology the Chinese experience has only proved my assertion that capitalism and Marxism are Western cousins.

While the only major surviving Marxist society is moving towards its cousin, the same is happening in many of the capitalist countries. They are moving away from traditional capitalism, cut and dried profit making, and being totally insensitive to social and humanitarian affects of their pursuit of profit making. In many countries, capitalists are trying to show sensitivity to humanitarian concerns and a concept of the welfare state is emerging. Meanwhile, Mao Tse-tung's thought, just like Islam, has become a counter philosophy to the dominant philosophy of globalization. In the Indian subcontintent, Marxists have become the dominant revolutionary force in Nepal, which is a traditional Hindu society. In the last couple of years, Maoist Naxalite movement has shown a big comeback. The chief minister of Andhra Pradesh narrowly survived an attack by the Naxalites. Combating Naxalism has become a top priority for the Indian government. Some of the Maoist groups have already started seeing parallels between their struggle and the struggle of Islamic fundamentalists. Both see globalization and its leader, America, as their main adversary.

Capitalism and Marxism may modify themselves, but they will not be able to solve the present crisis of globalization unless they recognize the spiritual aspect of life. This spiritual revival has to come from the East. Both these philosophies have failed to understand

Eastern philosophy. Both have based their theories on the Western experience alone and have declared that as the universal experience. This is the fundamental cause of the present crisis, the West has tried to impose its values on others as universal values. This tendency towards conformity has led to resentment and resistance among the others. When we present spiritual revival as the only solution to the present crisis, we also mean that only by fusing Western concepts with Eastern concepts we can have universal values. I believe we have to recognize that it is India, not China, which is the seat of Eastern spirituality and Guru Nanak's philosophy is the zenith of Eastern spirituality, chronologically the most developed form. If Marxism wants to be Easternized, then it has be be Indianized. To do that, it has to understand the message of Guru Nanak.

# CHAPTER SIX

## CONSUMERISM AND UTILITARIAN CAPITALISM

Today, we can clearly see divisions in the Western alliance. America is on one side and Europe and Canada are on the other. The widening gap between Europe and America, and between America and Canada, is not only due to competition in trade, but there is also an ideological basis for this phenomenon. England is still siding with the United States because of historical ties. England is the birthplace of capitalism. America is an ideological extension of England. In the nineteenth century and early part of twentieth century, England led the capitalist order in the world. Then it passed the baton to the United States.

America has become the leader of globalization, the highest developed form of capitalist order, but America has also started considering itself as the torch bearer of capitalism. America has developed a tendency to maintain the ideological purity of capitalism and wants to keep capitalism unadulterated. This puritan attitude has less to do with ideological purity than insecurity of losing the leader's place. America wants to hold on to the belief that if it modifies traditional capitalism, it risks disintegration of the capitalist camp. The Europeans and the Canadians have shown more flexibility in modifying traditional capitalism to meet the needs of their societies. American capitalism today is closer to the traditional capitalism and could be called consumerist capitalism while the European and the Canadian capitalism can be called utilitarian capitalism.

The division between consumerist and utilitarian capitalism is not watertight. America has also adopted its social welfare programs and Europeans are still making a lot of consumer goods and generating good profit. Their common currency, the Euro, is doing much better than the dollar, but still they continue to show more flexibility in dealing with domestic and international situations. While both America and Europe have consumerist and utilitarian elements in their economies, the consumerist element has been dominant in America while the utilitarian aspect is dominant in Europe.

Different historical, cultural, and social conditions have led to these differences. Europe has a long history and a relatively more stable culture. The social structure is also different than in America. Europe has seen ancient Greek and Roman civilizations, the rise of Christianity, Islamic invasions, renaissance, industrial revolution, French revolution, Paris commune, Russian revolution, and two world wars. Europe is the birth place of both capitalism and Marxism. The three components of Marxism, the British economy, French socialism, and German philosophy originated in Europe. Europe also experienced the evolution of distinct and stable national cultures.

Europe experienced many movements against the de-humanizing effects of capitalism. There was a sustained pressure on the European capitalists for making their system more responsive to humanitarian concerns and to the collective needs of society. All these factors contributed to make the European capitalists realize that they needed to modify their system. This led to the evolution of a concept of capitalism with a human face, or a social welfare state. This modified capitalism, in which the European capitalists made a compromise with their people to provide basic necessities and maintain a reasonable standard of life, can be called utilitarian capitalism. This change was made for the sake of political expediency rather than a real change of heart, because they treated people in their colonies very differently than people in their own countries. Concessions were given to their people, but people in the colonies were ruthlessly oppressed. None the less, it does show a degree of flexibility and political maturity to maintain a state of relative peace and harmony in their countries. The experience of getting along with their own people certainly helped them to show more flexibility than America in dealing with the developing countries of the third world.

America evolved very recently and does not have a long history. America has not had the time to develop a stable national culture. America hurriedly mixed different European cultures to quickly evolve a work ethic based on instant gratification. Moreover, there were some other unique features of the American society. Black people were brought as slaves long after slavery was abolished in other parts of the world. The lands of native Americans were acquired with such haste that due process was seldom possible. Large areas of Mexico were quickly incorporated into the United States. The European immigrants did not, in most cases, represent the mainstream in Europe. These people either could not make it in Europe or came to escape persecution. Some of them were exiled from their countries. People who could not make it in Europe were able to succeed in a very short time, mainly because of superabundant resources of this land. All these factors led to the belief that whatever system we have is the best and there was less pressure on the capitalists for change compared to their European counterparts. The philosophy of instant gratification also encouraged consumerist culture. All these factors were responsible for evolving consumerist capitalism.

The quick success also led to an arrogant attitude. We made it much faster than the Europeans. We beat them because we are more productive and we have more drive. The Europeans have lost steam. They have become lazy like lotus eaters in Greek mythology. I was shocked to hear sentiments like these expressed for the Europeans. I grew up in India where there was great respect for the Europeans. They were considered intelligent, hard working, and ingenious people who have made great progress. As a little boy in Patiala, my home town in India, I used to hear experiences of the Sikh soldiers who fought the Germans in the North African desert. They beat the troops of General Rommel, who was called "Desert Fox." They told me they had great respect for the Germans whom they were holding prisoners. They said these people were so smart they could fix anything such as a watch or a radio. If they had any problem with any of their machinery they would ask the Germans to help them fix it. They told me they always treated the German prisoners with respect and always wanted to do favors for them. If, on a special occasion, they would get some biscuits or candy, they would first offer those to the Germans.

Before World War II, Europe remained the center of Western civilization as well as the leading region and center of the capitalist and Marxist systems. After the second world war, Europe, which suffered massive destruction during the war, was temporarily pushed to the background by the United States. Even under those circumstances there were European leaders like Charles De Gaulle, who resented American leadership of Western civilization and of the capitalist system. There was large scale migration of people, including scientists, from Western Europe to the United States. These people gave a big boost to American science, technology, and research. They played a big role in making America the unchallenged leader of the West.

Meanwhile, the Soviet Union bounced back from the devastation of the war and its military industrial complex forged a formidable challenge to the West. The Western European countries were afraid of the Soviet tanks rolling over their countries and sought protection from America against the military might of the Soviet Union. This exaggerated the sense of arrogance in America which was already there.

To recover from the devastation and destruction of the war, the European countries realized they needed cooperation among themselves as well they needed participation of all sections of society. This was when European capitalism started deviating from American capitalism in a radical manner. Cooperation among the European countries led to the birth of the European Union and the European states embraced the concept of the social welfare state. These factors led to the emergence of utilitarian capitalism.

In the sixties, less than two decades after the war, Europe bounced back. Many Americans believe that America rebuilt Europe and Japan. But in Europe, one gets a very different perspective. One can only conclude that either Europeans are ungrateful or the belief of many Americans that massive American aid was the main factor in rebuilding Europe is exaggerated. European infrastructure and industrial base was more modern than the United States because during the second world war, the old infrastructure and industrial base were destroyed in Europe. By the seventies, Europe had already regained an economic lead. The European countries were still very afraid of the Soviet Union and continued to rely on American military might to counter the Soviet threat. Once the Soviet Union fell, in a strange way it hurt American interests more than any other country. On the surface, it appears that America gained a lot from the fall of the Soviet Union because it became the only superpower in the world, the unchallenged leader of the uni-polar world.

If you analyze in more depth, you will come to exactly the opposite conclusion. Western Europe, which was under American domination, had no reason to accept American domination. Fear of the Soviet Union was gone. Europe started demanding its traditional role as the leader of Western civilization. European economic might started posing a big challenge to America. China, which was kept under control by the Soviet Union, emerged as the leading power in Asia. After the fall of the Soviet Union, America became more arrogant and there was a feeling of national chauvinism and a shift to the right. All these factors led to the feeling that we are the greatest, our system is the best. In other words, consumerist capitalism is the best. America has been unable to see the other side of the picture. Being the only superpower leads to anti-American feelings in many parts of the world, including Europe. It also brings the unpleasant task of policing the whole world. By far the biggest damage has been the loss of incentive to modify consumerist capitalism to utilitarian capitalism, because of the misguided belief that we have emerged victorious.

One fact emerges when we compare consumerist capitalism with the utilitarian capitalism.Utilitarian capitalism has worked better for the majority of the people and consumerist capitalism favors a small minority. This leads to polarization of the society into have and have nots. Let us compare America with Western Europe. For the domestic policies, two areas are important to see what kind of services people are getting. One is health care and the other is education.

European countries are spending about 8% of GNP on health care, but they are getting better results in terms of overall health coverage of their population. All the population is covered. Two indexes of healthcare, infant mortality and maternal mortality, show that European countries are providing better coverage. America is spending about 15% of the G.N.P. but its infant and maternal mortality statistics do not match the Europeans. Moreover, forty three million Americans do not have any health coverage. Those people who can afford insurance get better care in America because in Europe you have to wait for your turn. Sometimes, the waiting period can run into several monthsfor a routine operation. In America, those people who can afford it, want their surgery done on the day they prefer, so they can fit it into their schedule better. Similarly, to have a CT scan or MRI, or other test, the wait can be considerable in Europe, whereas in America, those who can afford it can get it done on the day they want it, at least much sooner than in Canada or European countries.

In education, similar differences can be seen between consumerist and utilitarian capitalism. In Europe, good education is more accessible to the majority of people whereas in America, college education is much less likely for people from lower socio-economic strata. The drop out rate is much higher in the United States than in Europe. Research is also different in both societies. In Europe, research is mostly done for the collective interest of society. Generally, the research is sponsored by the state. In America, research is often sponsored by private corporations. Private corporations are more interested to advance their cause rather than the collective interest of society. The result has been that more research is being done in Europe. This phenomenon is also adversely affecting the educational standards.

For example, American high school students are far behind the students in other industrialized countries, particularly in math and science.

Crime and violence are other areas where there is a big difference in the two different types of capitalist societies. Crime, particularly violent crime, is many times higher in the United States than in European countries.

There is also a difference in foreign policy. Countries with utilitarian capitalism have generally shown more flexibility in their relations with other countries, particularly with developing countries. We can see the difference in American relations with Cuba as compared to relations of European countries and Canada with Cuba. Many European countries were able to keep better relations with their former colonies than America could maintain with its former client states after there was change in their governments or systems. Spain has still good relations with its former colonies in America. Great Britain has also maintained relations with its former colonies under the umbrella of commonwealth countries. France has maintained relations with its former colonies in Africa. Compare these relations with America's relations with Iran. At one time, the Shah of Iran was America's principle ally in the region, but after the Islamic revolution, America has been unable to maintain any kind of meaningful relations with Iran. Similarly, after the Communists took power in China European countries very quickly recognized the new government whereas America continued to recognize Taiwan for some twenty years, and it only recognized China when the whole world community expelled Taiwan from the United Nations and gave its seat to the People's Republic of China. It took America so much time to accept the simple fact that no country can afford not to have relations with the world's most populated country.

In conclusion, there is no watertight division between consumerist and utilitarian capitalism. There is plenty of overlapping. However, the European capitalists and to some extent the Canadian and Japanese capitalists have shown more flexibility in modifying some crude aspects of capitalism than American capitalists have shown. America has continued to consider itself the most pure, dedicated, and efficient follower of the traditional consumerist capitalism of free enterprise.

Americans seem to feel that those countries have become lethargic (victims of socialism) and inefficient, whereas America continues to march forward on the golden path of (true) traditional capitalism to new horizons of globalization, the highest stage of capitalist mode of production. America's leading role is cited as an example of the superiority of American consumerist capitalism. However, the victory lap may be premature. Globalization is running into increasing difficulties and anti-globalization sentiment is rising in the world. It may become a liability for America rather than its greatest asset.

For both capitalisms, profit making still remains the prime and ultimate goal. Both continue to have unrealistic faith and expectations in science and technology. They have not grasped the simple fact that science is a means but it cannot be the end. Science cannot decide what is right and what is wrong. This is the function of spirituality. Without spiritual revival, consumerist capitalists, utilitarian capitalists, and Marxists will all be unable to serve the interests of the vast majority of people. Not only that, without spirituality they will antagonize this vast majority. Capitalists and Marxists must show flexibility, even for the sake of their own survival, and accept the fact that by denying spirituality, they are negating the very essence of human society. Guru Nanak laid down the three basic principles for the proper functioning of society: honest work, sharing, and spiritual awakening.

# CHAPTER SEVEN

## EAST AND WEST—CHANGING EQUATIONS

In the last two centuries, under Western domination, Eastern philosophy, spirituality, secular concepts, and East's contribution in the overall development of humanity have mostly been ignored or denied. With the rise of the East in the twenty-first century, some questions have been raised. Is there any place for the Eastern concepts in resolving the crisis faced by the dominant Western society? Why could the technological and scientific development of the last two centuries not lead to similar progress in the humanitarian field? Many people feel that there has been a decline in human values during this period. Before the industrial revolution, the East had made more progress in almost every field.

After the industrial revolution, the West started leading in production. Because of this industrial growth, the West was able to conquer the East. This led to impoverishment, overpopulation, and decline in the environment of the East. Many Eastern intellectuals were influenced by this situation and started feeling that the East did not make any significant contribution to overall human development, and did not have much to offer in the contemporary world. This type of thinking was born out of a slavish mentality and inferiority complex. It denied the historical fact that barring the last two centuries, the East was the leading region.

What caused the East to play this leading role? I feel that a favorable climate was the main cause for the phenomenon. The favorable climatic conditions led to development in spiritual, philosophical, and scientific fields. The favorable climate also encouraged tendencies of sharing, tolerance, and coexistence. There was also a concept that renunciation is a higher value. In the West, on the other hand, the harsh climate led to a bitter struggle for survival, hoarding, intense competition, and a tendency to conquer. The climatic differences also explain the Eastern emphasis on stability and the Western attitude of adventure and mobility. These conditions were also responsible for the development of Eastern cultivational and Western prescriptive spirituality. The concepts of pleasure are also different. The Eastern concept laid more emphasis on the inner source of happiness and contentment. The Western concept was of a never-ending quest for happiness. The Eastern concept of happiness stresses that real pleasure lies in self-enlightenment or knowing your real self. Being alienated from oneself is the real cause of pain and suffering.

The West's never-ending quest for pleasure sometimes led to unnatural ways to seek it, such as "night life." Nature made days to work and nights to rest. Dazzling lights, deafening music, and getting drunk can hardly be called a relaxing experience. Women were projected more as objects of pleasure rather than mothers. Sex was commercialized as a commodity. In a Western dominated world, these attitudes became universal. Even in the Eastern countries, where women's aspect of being a mother was emphasized more, the traditional outlook was abandoned. One can see that attitude very clearly in India, where Bollywood, the Indian equivalent of Hollywood, has enthusiastically promoted these new values. India is paying very dearly for the Bollywoodization of its traditional values. Aids epidemic has hit India in a very big way.

The Western attitude of trying to conquer nature rather than coexist with it has led to the environmental damage, which was unheard of in the previous eras. It is the view of several environmentalists that our environment has been damaged more, and more plant and animal species have vanished from the earth in the last two centuries than at any other time. Eating habits and life styles of people were affected. Meat was promoted as having a higher quality of protein compared to vegetable proteins. This has resulted in a very unhealthy population. It is interesting to note that problems of being overweight and obesity have completely gotten out of control with the change in eating habits. Similarly, the status of mental health of the people can be estimated by the record number of antidepressants, tranquilizers, and hypnotics being used now as compared to any other time in history.

Now the trends have started changing. It is becoming clear that Western domination of the last two centuries is not going to last in this century. The twenty-first century is going to look very different than the last two centuries. Asia is going to become the leading region; China the largest economy, and Islam will emerge as the largest religion.

The intellectually enlightened segment of Western society has become aware of these trends. This phenomenon can be called "intellectual polarization." The gap between the intellectuals and the general population is becoming wider. Many intellectuals are being attracted to Eastern cultivational spirituality. A growing number of people are becoming vegetarian. Many are trying Eastern relaxation techniques such as yoga and meditation. The phenomenon of intellectual polarization also becomes apparent when we see that, on one hand, the mainstream America continues to consume more food and drink, and keeps adding pounds of adipose tissue (fat), but the intellectual segment is showing restraint in both eating and drinking. They are giving up hard liquor and starting to drink wine. Some drink mineral water during cocktail parties.

The more informed Americans have different views on foreign policy and generally are less likely to support war. Many of them support principles of pluralism, diversity, tolerance, and peaceful coexistence. They are also more likely to adopt better ideas from other cultures. The Eastern concepts of spirituality and overall human development are attracting many Westerners. They feel that their ideas can be a good resource for the rest of the world. In the last two centuries, these ideas were suppressed and therefore humanity could not benefit from them. Now, conditions have changed and these ideas are finding wider, even global acceptance. The ideas of tolerance, peaceful coexistence, harmony, pluralism, and diversity are very relevant and important for the contemporary world. The divisive "them against us" of seeing us separate from others must be overcome in the present day globalized world. Guru Nanak taught that we are parts of the whole, the feeling of otherness is the result of our ignorance. This ignorance comes from not realizing our true self. Once we realize our true identity, we can gain cosmic awareness and also become aware of universal brotherhood.

The Western domination of the last two centuries, in the final analysis, was dependant upon the economic strength of the West. The West felt its philosophy is better because it has worked, we are the richest. The East also conceded Western superiority because their thinking and system works better. That is why they are richer than us. If our philosophy or way of life was superior, then why are we poor and backward? Eastern lack of self confidence and inferiority compounded the problem of Western arrogance. These two feelings, the Eastern inferiority complex and Western arrogance, deprived the world of a more balanced outlook.

Science, technology and management techniques are better developed in the West, but spirituality and overall human development (physical, mental, and spiritual) did better in the East. Fusion of Western capitalism and Eastern spirituality can work better for both West and East. This is not going to happen until we get rid of Western arrogance and the Eastern inferiority complex. The only way this can be accomplished is by first accepting the fact that the Western economic lead is not an eternal phenomenon. The Western economic lead of the last two centuries does not amount to much compared to the thousands of years of the history of mankind,. Two centuries in the history of mankind are like two days in an individual's life. We may have two good days or two bad days; how much does that matter in the context of our whole life?

Even a very superficial analysis of the economic trend will reveal that economic equations between East and West are changing. This is becoming obvious that there is a net shift of power to the East. We can use different criteria, such as manufacturing, trade volume, number of consumers and emerging trade alliances. All of them point in the same direction, to the emerging strength of the East.

If we look at the steel production in the last three centuries, then one thing becomes obvious, steel production has been a fairly good indicator of the overall strength of a country or region. England was the leading steel producing country in the eighteenth and nineteenth centuries. Towards the end of the nineteenth century, Germany and America became big producers of steel, and this continued into the twentieth century. During World War II, the European steel industry was almost completely destroyed. America became the largest producer of steel in the world. In the '50s and '60s, Europe and Japan built new steel industries. The newly built European and Japanese steel industries were much more efficient than the older American steel industry. Europe and Japan quickly surpassed America in steel production.

If we analyze the steel production figures in the last decade, then some trends become obvious:

China has taken the first position and is now leading with a large margin.

American steel production continues to decline.

England does not even make it into last place of the top ten largest steel producers.

India and South Korea continue to produce more steel and their share of the world's production is continuously increasing.

Relatively, steel production has declined in western European countries compared to eastern European countries.

Over all, steel production is moving from the west to the east.

China is not only the biggest producer of steel, but is also the biggest consumer.

Another interesting fact can also be observed, that is, the steel production is also a good indicator of the overall performance of the economy of the country. For example, both China and India, which have shown a significant increase in steel production in the last decade, have also experienced a big rate of growth in their economies. For China, the rate of economic growth has been about 10% per year. The Indian economy has grown at a rate of more than 5% per year. China is now making about 30% of the world's steel.

Manufacturing is gradually shifting to Asia. Europe and then America led from the nineteenth century to twenty-first century. Asia is gradually increasing its share of manufacturing and is emerging as the leading region in manufacturing. China, Japan, Korea, and India are seeing their share of manufactured products growing compared to Europe and America. The same can be said of the trade volume. Asia is emerging as the major trade partner for both America and Europe. Trade is also running more in favor of Asia. For example, America's trade with China has shown a growing trade deficit in favor of China. Last year, this was more than 120 billion dollars.

One sees strains developing in Western economic and military alliances, but the Asian countries seem to be moving more towards unity. A growing gap can be seen between America and Canada. NATO seems to have outlived its purpose. The recent war in Iraq has brought differences between America and Europe, and America and Canada into the open. NATO could not take a united stand. Trade wars between America and Canada are becoming a rule rather than an exception. NAFTA (North America Free Trade Area) has performed miserably. Canada, America, and Mexico all seem to agree that NAFTA has not done much for them.

Compared to what is happening in the West, Asia seems to be moving in another direction. ASEAN (Association of Southeast Asian Nations) summit in Bali, Indonesia, last year showed that there is a real possibility in the near future for the emergence of the biggest trade alliance in the world, comprising both East Asia and South Asia. This may include Asian countries of China, Japan, Korea and India. This alliance will cover a population of more than three billion, half of the world's population. The recent summit of SARC (South Asian Regional Cooperation) in Islamabad, Pakistan (from Jan. 4 to Jan.6, 2004), also showed that the South Asian countries are moving towards unity and cooperation. These countries have a population which is about one fourth of the world's population (more than one and a half billion). Taiwan has just built the tallest building in the world, taller than the previously tallest one in Kulalumpur, Malaysia.

Politically, the major eastern countries are moving closer to each other. China, Russia, and India are moving towards formation of a strategic alliance. Relations between Russia and China and between China and India, which were very strained during the sixties and seventies, are constantly improving. Each of these three countries appeared to be moving closer to the West, but now they appear to have shifted gears and are looking to the East. The Indian and the Chinese leaders are using terms like Asia's Century. The recent election to Russian Duma showed that, for the first time in Russia, after the fall of the Soviet Union, pro-Western parties were unable to win a single seat. This fact alone can be indicative of the fact that Russia is tilting to the East.

These changes will lead to a relative decline of the Western influence and relative increase of Eastern influence. The relationship between the two will become more balanced. This situation will also lead to a change in attitude towards Eastern concepts. They will be taken more seriously as a resource for solving problems faced by the world and mankind. History presents new problems and we have to restate old principles in new ways to solve these problems. The Eastern concepts have seen unity in diversity and they see continuity and change as their main currents. Stability and change are not exclusive but coexist and are complementary.

Assimilation of the essential and positive elements of the other cultures is also an important Eastern concept. We have to reconcile economic, political, religious, and spiritual doctrines so that we can move forward together. We have to understand that what one culture regards as sound principles may be regarded as erroneous by the other cultures. Similarly, what is considered good by one culture may be considered evil by others. We have to understand that the meeting of East and West is the most important event of our time. This meeting has, on the one hand, led to a clash of civilizations, but on the other hand, it has also provided us an opportunity for synthesizing new values from the fusion of Eastern and Western values. These new values may become our biggest assets in meeting the challenges of globalization.

If we analyze Eastern and Western philosophies, the most fundamental difference is that the Eastern philosophy tends to be more comprehensive and all inclusive while the western philosophy shows a tendency towards compartmentalization. The Western philosophy lays more emphasis on specialization. There are many branches such as metaphysics, epistemology, logic, ethics, and aesthetics. There is a tendency to specialize in one of these branches and study that in more detail. The Eastern philosophers, on the other hand, were expected to address all of these. This can be called a synthetic outlook. There is the need for both detailed study of each aspect and grasp of the overall message in its totality. If we cannot bring fragmented knowledge together, then it will not serve any purpose. This will be like pieces of a jigsaw puzzle; unless they are properly put together, they will not make much sense.

In a Vedic story, six blind men went to feel an elephant and each described it depending upon which part of the elephant he felt. One who felt the trunk said it was like a snake. Another who felt the leg compared it to a pillar. Still another described it like a fan after feeling its ear. The fifth one felt the abdomen and said this was like a drum. The sixth felt its tail and said that was like a brush. They needed a man with eyes (man with a vision) to make sense of their different experiences.

The Indian philosophy aims at knowing the truth. This is termed the vision of truth *(darsan)*. All Indian schools of philosophies believed there can be a direct realization of truth *(Tat darsan)*. It can be called knowing the essence of truth. In other words, moving in the direction of knowing ultimate reality. The different schools of philosophy challenged each other and they were also challenged by skeptic, agnostic, and materialist charvaks. Charvaks in India were like Epicureans in Greece; they challenged the mainstream philosophy. We should not be afraid of being challenged for our convictions and beliefs. Such challenges actually help us by preventing us from becoming dogmatic.

In an era of globalization, different cultures have been brought face to face through the growth in transportation and communication. Our commonly held beliefs and ideas are being challenged. This is not necessarily a bad thing and could even be a good thing for all of us. This provides an opportunity to test our own ideas and beliefs while we have an opportunity to learn other perspectives. Guru Nanak traveled more than ten thousand miles on foot. He engaged other people who had different beliefs and different ideas in a dialogue. Guru Nanak preached a philosophy of dialogue more than five hundred years ago. In this age of globalization, dialogue assumes a central role, particularly between East and West. With changing equations between East and West, old ways of the West, which were developed in an era of Western domination, may not be useful and even can prove harmful. We have to change our old ways and adapt them to the new conditions.

# CHAPTER EIGHT

## GLOBALIZATION VERSUS A GLOBAL COMMUNITY

With the growth of the means of transportation and communication, we have globalized the world. But this globalization is economic globalization only, which means that the world has been developed as one large market. There is no social, cultural, or moral globalization. By social, I mean that there is no concern for the social effects of the globalization and by cultural, I mean that there is no conception in the present globalization to address how different cultures will react to each other. There is no concept of looking at different cultures as a rich resource to find solutions to the challenges we face as a world community. The lack of moral concept means that the present globalization has no concern for what is right and what is wrong. The lack of social, cultural, and moral aspects in globalization means that we have a globalization without a global perspective. The present globalization is the highest stage of imperialism, or the highest stage of consumerist capitalism. Its only concern is to extend its markets and profits to the maximum without any concern as to how it will effect the people and how it will effect the planet.

I had the opportunity to see the results of globalization both in America and India, a developing country of the third world. In both societies, the negative effects of globalization outweigh the positive ones. There is increased polarization of the societies. The gap between the rich and the poor has widened. The benefits of globalization have not filtered down to the vast majority of people and have been usurped by the elite. Already existing social benefits have either been withdrawn or have been diluted. As a result of this policy, healthcare and education for the poor and lower middle class have suffered tremendously. The middle class has been eroded, a small segment of the upper middle class has benefited from globalization and has joined the ranks of the rich, while a larger sector, the lower middle class, has been squeezed to join the poor. The middle class provided a degree of stability to society. The erosion of the middle class has led to destabilization.

In the thirty years I have lived in America, I have seen the maximum impact of globalization. In the early seventies, American workers were more productive and were getting more wages than the European workers. In 1971, I did my internship in a hospital in South Chicago. The hospital was in a white working class neighborhood. Many people there worked in the steel mills in Gary and Hammond, Indiana, which were only a few miles away. Many patients invited me to their homes to have dinner with them. I was amazed. They had big and comfortable cars, color television, and the furniture and crockery were very impressive. They had things which only very rich people could afford in India, except that at that time there was no color TV in India. Some of these people told me that they were making about fifteen dollars an hour, which I think is equivalent to about fifty dollars now. They were able to send their children to colleges and universities.

I went back a few times to revisit the area. The neighborhood was completely changed. Most of the white people, whoever could afford it, left the area; mostly black and Hispanic people moved in. Each time I went back, the area looked more run down than before. I was doing my residency in a hospital in Philadelphia in an area which catered to the white middle class. Compared to this, my previous hospital and area looked very run down. After finishing my residency I worked in a hospital in Montgomery County, next to Philadelphia. This was in an area where upper middle class and rich people lived. I used to go back to the other hospital where I did my residency, and got the same feeling which I had when I used to go back to Chicago from Philadelphia.

In the late eighties, I moved to the central part of Washington State. One thing which struck me was that there were so many white people on welfare. In the Mid-West and on the East Coast, I was under the impression that only blacks and Hispanics were on welfare. This was my first experience with white people on welfare. The other thing which struck me was that the other white people were neither more sympathetic nor kinder to these people. As a matter of fact, I saw more prejudice against these people and more derogatory words used for these poor white people than I had heard for black and Hispanic people who were on welfare in the East and Midwest. Since we moved to the central part of Washington State, we have seen a large influx of the Hispanic people. They are the poorest people now in the area. They bear the brunt of unkind and derogatory words. In the Midwest and East Coast, I had never heard those derogatory words and was not aware that there was such a strong prejudice against the Hispanics. It appears that they had reserved most of their prejudice against the black people.

I feel my experiences are not isolated or individual experiences, but reflected the changes brought by globalization to this country. America has come a long way from the white working class to the lowest standard of living of the farm workers, and most of them happen to be Hispanics. My initial impression of America has changed tremendously in the last thirty years. The living standards of the white working class first appeared to me equivalent to the rich in India. Now, the living standard of the poor Hispanics in central Washington area can be compared to poor people in the third world countries. There is however another side of the story. Many Indian doctors and other people who owned businesses used to own simple cars and reasonably comfortable houses. Now, these people have elegant cars and palatial houses.

One could drive from Philadelphia to Atlantic City in the early seventies and see farms and orchards, but now you only see concrete jungles and start wondering why New Jersey is called the Garden State? In 1972, when I first drove from Los Angeles to Anaheim to see Disneyland there were actually orange groves, but now, it is a solid concrete mass. Walt Disney must be turning in his grave to see his Disneyland surrounded by giant concrete mountains (big hotel buildings) surrounding his dream retreat from the big cities. These buildings seem to be mocking at the whole idea of Walt Disney and appear like monuments to Capitalist greed. The Disney World in Orlando, Florida, has also come a long way. I first saw it in 1972 when it was just opened, and the last time I saw it was in 1995; I have no desire to go back. I'd rather retain my original pleasant memories than be shocked by present realities.

America is more polarized, more congested, and large areas of America are being ghetto-ized. America is the only industrialized country which is rapidly gaining population. It is estimated that at the end of this century, America's population will reach a billion. For the vast majority of people, that can mean a journey from the first world (top of the world) to the third world. Americans will not have to travel to third world countries to see poverty, deprivation, illiteracy, and destitution; they will have the convenience of watching that right here. The European workers in many West European countries have already become more productive than the American workers, and their wages have also exceeded the American workers. Forty-three million Americans have no health coverage. We are way behind the other industrialized societies in the field of education, particularly mathematics and science. What we lost intellectually we have gained physically. We are the fattest people and are still growing fatter.

I frequently travel to India and stay most of the time in Punjab, which is my home state. The picture of globalization is not only equally depressing but much more desperate. There are few posh colonies springing up in big cities and there are more cars and color televisions. But for the majority of the people, life has become worse. There is so much congestion in the cities and on the highways. The infrastructure of the cities is breaking down. There is so much filth in the big cities. The railway lines in all big cities have been hijacked by the poor people who use them as open toilets and for their living quarters. Water is becoming a scarce commodity. Clean air in the big cities is a luxury. Many rivers have become like sewage drains. There is rapid deforestation. Many animal species have disappeared. In Punjab and some neighboring states, the area covered by forests is less than four percent. Even in that small area many trees are decaying or dying, and even tough birds like vultures are dying. All this terrible pollution hits really bad in winter months when fog sometimes brings life almost to a complete halt, planes cannot land and trains and traffic on the roads have to stop because of low visibility.

The ill effects of globalization are not limited to environmental damage alone. There are moral and cultural effects. Rapid urbanization and increased mobilization have led to social destabilization. Globalization has promoted a global consumer culture which encourages people to make money the quickest and the easiest way. This consumerist global culture has suppressed other cultures. The cultural values of people have been eroded. This leads to cultural instability. Social destabilization and cultural instability have made people unstable and vulnerable. These factors lead to drugs, prostitution, crime, violence and are responsible for the AIDS epidemic.

After the so-called green revolution globalized Punjab's agrarian economy, social and cultural problems also quickly followed. In addition to all the problems already mentioned, there are problems which have particularly affected women. These problems are: female feticide, fake marriage, and becoming widows at a young age. Under the influence of consumerist global culture, people want to make decisions primarily based on monetary factor. Birth of a female child is considered a loss because you have to give a dowry while a male child will bring a dowry. Why not get rid of a female infant and avoid your loss? Globalization also made technology like fetal ultrasound available. The result was that female feticide became a very big problem in Punjab. Punjab has the lowest female to male ratio in India. Even though female infanticide was practiced in the feudal times, it was done in a very limited manner, and the practice never became widespread. After globalization, the problem has really become a big social problem in Punjab. The problem of fake marriages has also become very widespread in Punjab. Marriages are now being arranged primarily for gaining immigration to the Western countries. The institution of marriage has been thoroughly commercialized. Thousands of fake marriages are performed. There are thousands of women in Punjab who have become victims of the fake marriage. These women were promised immigration to the West after marriage but they find out they have been cheated. With increased congestion on the roads, accidents have increased many times over. Many men are killed in these accidents, leaving behind widows. There are thousands of such widows in Punjab.

The social and cultural effects of globalization are resulting in growing tensions between different cultures. The different cultures feel threatened from the consumerist global culture and they are fighting back. Islamic culture has become the present opponent of the consumerist global culture. The clash between these two cultures has already destabilized the world, but confrontation between them can be even more dangerous.

What can we do to avoid the ill effects of globalization? One thing we cannot do is to go back to our way of life before the globalization era. The technology, like the internet, has already integrated us. We have to go forward since we cannot go back. Science and technology are not at fault. If they are used properly, for the benefit of the vast majority of people on this planet, then they can be very useful. *The main problem with the present globalization is that it lacks a global perspective. If we can provide what is lacking, then we can have a global community.* We have to look around to see where we may find an ideology which can provide us with this global perspective.

Guru Nanak's message is suited to impart a global perspective to globalization. Guru Nanak had a universal outlook and a global perspective. He envisioned a global community more than five hundred years ago based on the principles of love, tolerance, peaceful coexistence, pluralism, diversity, universal concern, and universal well being. These principles can make the present globalization responsive to social, cultural, and moral concerns.

If globalization becomes sensitive to these concerns, then it will no longer be limited to the economic aspect and will be all-inclusive, leading to a global community in the true sense.

At present, anti-globalization forces include students and other intellectuals, labor, environmentalists, and human rights activists. All of these groups are opposing globalization because they feel globalization is not addressing social, humanitarian and environmental issues, and is limited to economic globalization. These groups also feel that the economic benefits of globalization have not reached the majority of people. We have to see that anti-globalization forces have a much broader base than anti-Vietnam war forces. During the Vietnam war, the anti-war forces had students and intellectuals, but working people were not with them. This time students, intellectuals, and labor (working people) are on the same side. This makes the front more broad based and potentially much stronger. If globalization ignores their concerns, then it can get into a much greater problem than it already has. On the other hand, if globalization can acquire a global perspective, then all these anti-globalization forces can become its ardent supporters. Many people who are opposed to the present globalization are advocates of a global community. They are not opposed to scientific and technological progress. They do not want to turn the clock back. They want the benefits of scientific progress and technological advancement shared by the vast majority of people. They are not opposed to the integration of people; they are opposing the assimilation of people. There is a difference between integration and assimilation. Integration is more voluntary than forced, and there is coming together without losing one's identity. Assimilation is more forced and less voluntary, and one's independent identity is lost.

There is unity in diversity with integration, but assimilation creates the dissolution of diversity without achieving unity.

Advances in technology can sometimes move things in a different direction than the corporate greed had intended. The multinational corporations in the developed countries had convinced people in their countries that they want to move unclean manufacturing jobs to the developing countries because they pollute the environment. Once the corporations saw opportunity to extract profit from "clean jobs," they could not resist the temptation of making more profit, proving once again that globalization is the highest stage of consumerist capitalism. This new phenomenon of exporting clean jobs is called outsourcing. India, with its large knowledge of the English language and a large work force, is becoming the main beneficiary of this outsourcing. Many jobs related to typing and dictation and other similar work will be exported to India. There is a difference between globalization and a global community. In globalization, these decisions are based on corporate greed, but if we have a global perspective, then we can use the world's resources in a planned manner for the benefit of the majority of people.

The Iraq war is another typical example of corporate greed. Iraq had no weapons of mass destruction, and did not pose a threat to the security of United States. Saddam Hussein had no links with terrorists. Controlling the Middle East's oil was the goal. The war provided an opportunity for corporations to make money by selling weapons for unnecessary destruction and then give them an opportunity to rebuild what was destroyed.

The war brought Islamists into Iraq who were kept out by Saddam. The Iraq war is going to force increasing opposition all over the world because it is going to bring anti-war and anti-globalization forces together. In the end, the Iraq war may prove to be a significant step in the transition of globalization to a global community.

Globalization, which was limited to economic globalization and envisioned converting the whole world into one huge market while making people only consumers, is running into difficulties. This unbridled corporate greed is creating very serious social, cultural, environmental, and political problems. These problems are bringing together many forces which are opposing globalization for one reason or another. The more globalization is expanding, the more opposition and resistance it is running into. The only way out of this mess is to impart a global perspective to the current globalization. Guru Nanak's message becomes very relevant and important because out of different ideologies available to us, Guru Nanak's message has more potential to provide us with a global perspective, which we are lacking.

# CHAPTER NINE

## GURU NANAK'S MESSAGE OF THE UNITY OF MANKIND

Guru Nanak, the founder of the Sikh religion, was a great humanitarian and there is no doubt in my mind that history will judge him as the most important person of the second millenium. Guru Nanak had the broadest vision among all the visionaries. He was the strongest advocate of a global community. His concept of a global community was all-inclusive. It included all human beings, all living organisms, and non-living objects. Guru Nanak's message of the unity of mankind was based on the principle that there is only one creator for all human beings, living organisms, and non-living objects. Therefore, they are all inter-related. All are children of the same creator. Therefore, they are inter-related and are equal. Guru Nanak asks how can it be that He, the creator, has created some good and bad people or superior or inferior people? Guru Nanak said it is our ignorance which separates us from the others. When that curtain of ignorance is lifted with real knowledge, then the feeling of separation is gone and we realize we are part of the whole. We merge with the whole as a drop merges with the ocean. As long as the drop feels it is a separate entity, it will have a feeling of smallness and insecurity, which generates fear and anxiety. When the drop realizes that its content, regardless of its size, is water, which is the same content of the ocean, then it overcomes the feelings of insecurity, anxiety, and fear by recognizing the vastness of its existence. When we recognize the essence of our existence, we are united with all-pervasive reality. In other words, when we realize our true self, then we achieve a level of cosmic and universal existence. All our fears and anxieties are gone and we achieve a supreme status and find ourselves in a state of supreme bliss.

There are different ideologies which give a message of unity of mankind, but Guru Nanak's message is most logical, most emphatic, and most clear. The Sikh holy book, *Guru Granth Sahib,* which was established in the year 1604 (2004 is the 400th anniversary), starts with an analysis and comprehension of the number "one." This primal number is the universal creator and the fundamental principle *(Mool Mantar)* is the definition of the universal creator. In my humble opinion *Guru Granth Sahib* is the extension of the *Mool Mantar;* in other words, it explains the idea of oneness. Therefore, unity of mankind is the central theme of *Guru Granth Sahib.* Other-ness, the feeling of separation from others, is a product of our ignorance. There is only one ultimate reality, the eternal truth, which is the source of all other realities. This unchanging and eternal reality is beyond the reach of our senses since it is infinite and our senses can only reach things which have limits and boundaries (the finite dimension). This is called *Nirgun* (transcendent). It is called *Parbrahm* and *Parmesar* meaning beyond *Brahm,* and the Supreme Good. This transcendent ultimate reality manifests itself in nature, which is its creation, in a form which is called *Sargun* (immanent). Nature is the perceptive reality which we can feel around us, but there is no separation of this reality from the ultimate reality. Ultimate reality manifests itself in the immanent (perceptive) reality. Those who feel that creator and creation are two separate realities, or God and nature as two separate realities, are feeling this because of their ignorance. Any philosophy which sees two separate realities is promoting dualism or parallelism should be considered the product of ignorance.

The way to realize ultimate reality, the eternal truth, is by realizing our true self, because that ultimate reality, the eternal truth, is manifested in each one of us. The realization of true self is the way to cosmic consciousness and universal existence. This will lead to unity and supreme bliss while ignorance of ultimate reality will lead to separation, insecurity, anxiety and fear. This will also lead to fear and suffering because you will be constantly torn apart by feelings of *Rag* and *Divesh,* meaning attachment and repulsion.

The way of uniting (merging) with ultimate reality is the way of love and knowledge. Love and knowledge will go together whereas hatred and ignorance will also accompany each other. Love is born out of the feelings of oneness and unity which in turn promotes love. Feelings of oneness and unity are products of knowledge. Therefore, there is relationship between love and knowledge. The harmonious integration of heart with mind, the synthesis of the female and male principles, establishes a wholeness of being, uniting love and knowledge, which is the wisdom of the liberated soul, abiding in the bliss of perfect peace and divine joy.

Guru Nanak calls the individual soul as soul bride which wants to unite with its husband, the supreme soul *(Parmatma),* God. Love between *Jeevatma* (individual soul) and supreme soul *(Parmatma)* leads us to merge with the ultimate reality. Guru Nanak compares us with females because females are more receptive. They are geophysical, with dominance of heart whereas males are astrophysical, with dominance of the head. Knowledge elevates us to a level where we can become receptive for the ultimate merger. This is a stage where we can feel the *Shabad* in our heart. The *Shabad* translates into Word, meaning the word of God, but it is more than a word; it is a vibration. This vibration is going to be felt more by a heart-dominated person. In other words, for the merger as uniting with ultimate reality eternal truth), we have to transcend body, mind, and intellect, and feel with our heart (soul). Love is the ultimate vehicle for this union, but to reach the level of unity, we need the highest level of knowledge, *Tat gian* (essence of knowledge) or *Braham gian* (spiritual knowledge). At that level, knowledge and love will fuse with each other.

Guru Nanak's concept of God was a merciful, compassionate and forgiving one. This concept was different than the Judeo-Semitic one in which God is both compassionate and forgiving but also shows wrath and punishes. Guru Nanak said that our punishment is our separation from God, which is the cause of our pain and suffering. The moment we realize our true self and unite with God, He forgives all our mistakes and sin. Guru Nanak also differed from the karma philosophy of the Hindu religion, which believes that we will be held accountable for actions (karma) by God and like each action has a reaction, all our karmas have to be rewarded or punished depending upon whether they are good or bad karmas. If our karma cannot be accounted for in this birth, then we will have to be reborn to face the consequences of our karmas. Guru Nanak said that when we realize our true self and merge with God, all our karmas are resolved and we are liberated. We do not have to be reborn. Guru Nanak's philosophy is of optimism *(chardi kala)*. There is always hope for your salvation, no matter how many mistakes you have made, so long as you are willing to come to the sanctuary of God, you will be saved.

Guru Nanak was a great advocate of pluralism and diversity. He preached that there is more than one way to reach the eternal truth (God). When he was asked which religion was better, Hindu or Muslim, he replied that what really matters is that one becomes a good human being. The holy book of the Sikhs, *Guru Granth Sahib,* is truly a multicultural holy book. Words from many languages, including Punjabi, Sanskrit, Bengali, Marathi, Farsi (Persian), and Arabic have been used. Besides linguistic diversity there is religious diversity also. In addition to the writings of the Sikh gurus, the writings of Hindu saints *(Bhagats)* and Muslims (Sufis) are also included. The message of Guru Nanak is not limited to any religion, caste, nation, country, race, or color. His message was for all mankind. The message of *Guru Granth Sahib* is the message of unity of mankind.

Guru Nanak advocated the principle of dialogue between differing viewpoints. This philosophy promotes tolerance and peaceful coexistence. Guru Nanak traveled ten thousand miles on foot and engaged in a dialogue with many scholars and followers of many faiths, including different sects of Hindus and Muslims.

Guru Nanak condemned rituals and advocated essence of knowledge (spiritual knowledge) and enlightenment as means of salvation. Religious leaders, both Hindus and Muslims, at that time had become corrupt and were misleading people. These leaders were maintaining their control over the people by promoting only rituals and not preaching the real principles of Hinduism or Islam. Guru Nanak tried to free people from rituals and asked that people follow the real principles of their religions. He wanted Hindus to become good Hindus and Muslims good Muslims. Above all, he wanted people to become good human beings.

Guru Nanak stood for equality and social justice. He condemned all kinds of divisions among men if based on caste, color, or creed. He said all men are created equal. One time, he was invited to a feast given by a very rich and powerful ruler but instead he chose to stay with an honest working man. The rich man got very upset and asked Guru Nanak why he rejected his invitation and ate the poor workingman's food. Guru Nanak explained to him that, "You exploit other people and suck their blood. Therefore, your food is like the blood of the exploited people, whereas the poor workingman's bread contains milk of his honest labor."

Guru Nanak strongly opposed all kinds of exploitation and discrimination such as those based on socio-economic status, religious beliefs, or gender. He said if somebody exploits somebody else or violates their rights, then for that person, if he is a Hindu, it is like eating cow, and if he is Muslim, it is equivalent to eating pork (pig). He condemned the discrimination against women and rejected any suggestion that women were inferior to men. He asked, "How can women be inferior when they give birth to kings and all great men?"

Guru Nanak promoted the concept of a balanced life. While accepting the traditional fundamental principles of Eastern cultivational spirituality, that self-realization is the ultimate goal of spiritual growth, he preached that self realization cannot be done by renunciation and getting isolated from society. It has to be done while fulfilling your social obligations. He preached that social interaction is a must for one's spiritual awakening. He laid great emphasis on company with good people, *Sadh Sangat,* which can also be translated as congregation. Guru Nanak held a dialogue with Sidhas, a sect of spiritual people who had renounced society and had retreated to the jungle and mountains, in order to concentrate on their spiritual growth. Guru Nanak explained to them that their approach was not right because if spiritually awakened people leave society, then who will take care of it? He said one's own spiritual growth was not possible without fulfilling one's social obligations. Guru Nanak tried to balance individualistic spiritual tendency of Hinduism with a collective perspective of Islam on spirituality. Islam lays a strong emphasis on the social obligations for an individual's spiritual growth. The concept of *Zaikat* and *Jihad,* in my understanding, are collective perspectives of spirituality. *Zaikat* means sharing your wealth with other needy people. The word *Jihad,* which can also be interpreted as holy war, but I feel this has a broader connotation, meaning collective struggle for spiritual purification.

Guru Nanak preached that for your spiritual awakening, you should not deny or renounce the material reality. Nature is material reality, but it was created by the creator, the eternal truth (ultimate reality). Therefore, the creator, who is manifested in nature, is omnipresent. In other words, material reality is not separate from the creator (ultimate reality). Those who deny material reality or consider it separate from the ultimate reality are ignorant, or are promoting parallelism or dualism. Guru Nanak condemned all forms of parallelism and dualism.

We are also part of the creation (material or perceptive reality). We cannot ignore it or deny it but should help transform it along with our spiritual growth. The society is a material reality; whatever is happening to it we cannot stay aloof and be apathetic about it because whatever is happening to society will affect us and we in turn can affect society. Guru Nanak's philosophy therefore is of both individual spiritual growth and social transformation. Guru Nanak condemned in the strongest words possible political corruption, religious hypocrisy, and social degeneration during his time. His philosophy laid the foundation for a unique, continuous, and complete revolution, called the Sikh religion. As opposed to Marxism, which takes a class of society as the fundamental unit for transformational revolution, the Sikh religion takes the individual as the fundamental unit for transformation. In other words, the Sikh religion wanted to create a new man. These new men will then transform society. Guru Gobind Singh, the tenth guru of the Sikhs, gave a practical shape to Guru Nanak's philosophy and created *Khalsa.* The word *Khalsa* means pure and sovereign. *Khalsa* is a sovereign army of God. These people have reached the highest spiritual level. Therefore, they have merged with God, but as God's army, they engage in wiping out all kinds of oppression, exploitation, discrimination, and corruption.

*Khalsa* is not an army of any individual, religion, nation, country, or region. *Khalsa* is an embodiment of Guru Nanak's concept of a global community. Guru Nanak conceives of an all-inclusive community where nobody is excluded or left out. The basis of this community is Guru Nanak's philosophy of the unity of mankind. We all are children of the same God. We have been created from the same source, the eternal truth (ultimate reality,) the constant creator. Not only men, but all other living organisms and non-living objects have been also created from the same source. Therefore, Guru Nanak's concept of a global community is not limited only to men, but also includes all other living organisms and non-living objects because all of them have been created from the same source. Guru Nanak calls this global community *Sarbat.* This global community is based on his global perspective and universal outlook. This community is being maintained by a universal order which Guru Nanak called *Hukam.* All components of this global community are maintained in a state of dynamic balance by this universal order. Each component of the global community has a special role in maintaining ecological balance. Therefore, man has to live in harmony with nature. If we try to conquer nature, then we will break the dynamic ecological balance and will end up paying very dearly for the consequences of our actions.

We are already beginning to see some of the consequences of our actions, based on the policies of present globalization which are motivated by selfishness and greed. Environmental degradation, global warming, social destabilization, wars for controlling resources of other countries, disintegration of families, decline of moral and ethical values, increasing crime and violence, and AIDS are some of the consequences of our actions.

Guru Nanak had three principles for this global community: honest work, sharing, and spiritual awakening. People have to engage in honest work for the running of a society. You should not cheat others and you should not exploit others. As you work honestly and make your contribution to the functioning of society, all can prosper. By sharing, you are addressing the needs of society because all people cannot perform equal amount of work, but they still have needs. For example, people who are handicapped or people with more dependents may need help from others. In a spirit of sharing, we can fulfill needs of all members of society. If all people do honest work according to their capability, and if everybody's needs are taken care of, then the society can function in the best and most efficient way.

This was exactly the utopian goal of Marxism and communism, but it did not work because something was missing in the equation— the concept of right or wrong. Who is going to be the judge of what is right and what is wrong? Guru Nanak brings the third dimension, the spiritual awakening, which was denied by both Marxism and capitalism. Society has to address the issue of right and wrong. There are ethical and moral issues. What is the best way to decide right from wrong, and what is the best way of enforcing the right? It can be done either by imposing force from outside (prescriptive spirituality), or by evolving from inside (cultivational spirituality). In general, anything which evolves is superior to anything which is imposed. If people are spiritually awakened, then they can decide right from wrong. Our historical experience so far has shown that trying to force these concepts has not worked because the enforcing authorities become corrupt themselves.

Even if we created a class of spiritually awakened people which is given the task of enforcing these concepts, such as Brahmins in the Indian caste society, then that class also can become an intellectual elite and eventually, a corrupt class. Therefore, Guru Nanak was opposed to all kinds of elitism and wanted this global community to be based on principles of equality and social justice. To accomplish this goal, he advocated spiritual awakening of the masses, of all members of society.

Guru Nanak showed how the priestly classes become elitist, divorce themselves from the masses, and become corrupt. They promoted ritualism and deprived the masses of real spiritual knowledge. Guru Nanak condemned ritualism and exposed corruption and hypocrisy of the priestly classes. He bypassed them and took his message directly to the masses. One way of doing this was using people's own spoken language, Punjabi, for spreading his message. Guru Nanak preached that humility is the highest virtue and arrogance is the biggest vice. Humility leads to knowledge and arrogance leads to ignorance.

The three pillars of a global community, honest work, sharing and spiritual awakening are called *Kirat Karo* (honest work), *Wand Chako* (sharing), and *Nam Japo* (spiritual awakening). Like all true revolutionaries, Guru Nanak was optimistic. He says *"Nanak Nam Charhdi Kala, Tere Bhane Sarbat Da Bhala."* This means that by spiritual awakening, we become optimistic and we pray for universal well-being (welfare of the global community).

Bhai Gurdas, a great Sikh scholar, called Guru Nanak the spiritual leader of the world. He told the Hindus he was like the sacred river Ganges, and to the Muslims, was like their holy city, Mecca. He said that Guru Nanak unified people belonging to all four castes and came to liberate the oppressed and the downtrodden people of the earth. Bhai Gurdas said that Guru Nanak is supreme among the spiritual leaders. He was like a sun whose light dispelled the darkness of ignorance from the world.

The effects of Guru Nanak's message of unity of mankind is evident from this story associated with Guru Nanak's death. After his death, both Hindus and Muslims claimed his body and started fighting over it. Hindus said that he was a Hindu because he was born in a Hindu family. Muslims said that he was a Muslim because he performed Haj, the holy pilgrimage to Mecca. The legend has it that when they removed the shroud, instead of a dead body, there were flowers. The Hindus and Muslims divided the flowers. Hindus cremated them, and Muslims buried them.

Guru Nanak's message of unity of mankind can provide us with the global perspective that we badly need. Guru Nanak's message comes from the zenith of Eastern cultivational spirituality, and is also the essence of Eastern thought. The West should seriously and sincerely look at the Eastern philosophy. The fusion of Western capitalism with Eastern spirituality may help us in moving towards a global community. Guru Nanak's message, based upon principles of love, tolerance, peaceful coexistence, pluralism, diversity, universal concern, universal well-being, equality, social justice, struggle against oppression, eliminating exploitation and all kinds of discrimination, and unity of mankind, has the potential for becoming our greatest asset in our march towards a global community.

# SELECT LIST OF REFERENCES
## FOR RELATED READING AND STUDY

**Albert, Michael.** *Parecon: Life After Capitalism (Particapatory Economics) 2003*

**(Sri) Aurobindo Ghose.** *The Life Divine. 2 vols. 10$^{th}$ ed., 1977*
*The Synthesis of Yoga. 6$^{th}$ ed., 1976*

**Brown, Lester.** *Plan B: Rescuing A Planet Under Stress and A Civilization In Trouble*

**Chomsky, Noam.** *Hegemony or Survival: America's Quest for Dominance. 2003*

**Coomaraswami, Ananda K.** *What Is Civilisation? And Other Essays 1989*

**Cousens, Gabriel M.D.** *Sevenfold Peace: World Peace Through Body, Mind, Family, Community, Culture, Ecology, God. 1990-*

**Dorn, A. Walter, ed.** *World Order For A New Millennium 1999*

**Elgin, Duane.** *Promise Ahead: A Vision, of Hope and Action For Humanity's Future 2000*

**Feuerstein, Georg.** *Wholeness or Transcendence: Ancient Lessons for the Emerging Global Civilization 1992*

**Hawkins, David R. M.D. Ph.D.** *Power vs. Force: An Anatomy of Consciousness 2002*
*The Eye of the I: From Which Nothing Is Hidden 2003*
*Reality and Subjectivity 2003*

**Hocking, William Ernest.** *The Coming World Civilization 1956*

**Houston, Jean.** *Life Force: the Psycho-Historical Recovery of the Self 1993*

**Hubbard, Barbara Marx.** *Conscious Evolution: Awakening the Power of our Social Potential 1998*

**Jaspers, Karl.** *The Origin and Goal of History 1953*

**Lerner, Michael.** *The Politics of Meaning 1996*

**Matter, Joseph Allen.** *Love, Altruism, and the World Crisis: the Challenge of Pitirim Sorokin 1974*

**McLaughlin,Corrinne & Gordon Davidson, eds.,** *Spiritual Politics: Changing the World from the Inside Out 1994*

**Mumford, Lewis.** *"The Human Prospects," pp.161-184, in The Transformations of Man 1962*

**Nasr, Seyyed Hossein.** *Knowledge and the Sacred 1989 (the Gifford Lectures 1981)*

**Northrop, F.S.C.** *The Meeting of East and West 1960*

**Reiser, Oliver.** *Cosmic Humanism: A Theory of the Eight-Dimensional Cosmos Based On Integrative Principles From Science, Religion, and Art 1966*

**Russell, Walter.** *The Secret Of Light 1994 (*based upon his inspired 2 vol. The Divine Iliad)*

**Schimmel, Annemarie.** *Mystical Dimensions of Islam 1975*

**Schuon, Frithjof.** *The Transcendent Unity of All Religions 1984*

**Schweitzer, Albert.** *The Philosophy of Civilization 1960*

**Singh, Sawraj M.D.** *The Crisis in Civilization: A Sikh Perspective 2001*

**Singh, Trilochan, et al.** *The Sacred Writings of the Sikhs. UNESCO 1998*

**Tagore, Rabindranath.** *The Religion of Man 1931 (the Hibbert Lectures, Oxford, 1930)*

**Thompson, Wm Irwin.** *Coming Into Being: Artifacts & Texts in the Evolution of Consciousness 1996*

**Toynbee, Arnold J.** *An Historian's Approach to Religion 1950 (Gifford Lectures, Oxford, 1952-3)*

**Williamson, Marianne, ed.** *Imagine What America Could Be In the 21st Century Visions of a Better Future from Leading American Thinkers 2000*